History and the Internet: A Guide

History and the Internet: A Guide

By Patrick D. Reagan, Ph.D.
Tennessee Technological University

Boston   Burr Ridge, IL   Dubuque, IA   Madison, WI   New York
San Francisco   St. Louis   Bangkok   Bogotá   Caracas   Kuala Lumpur
Lisbon   London   Madrid   Mexico City   Milan   Montreal   New Delhi
Santiago   Seoul   Singapore   Sydney   Taipei   Toronto

McGraw-Hill Higher Education

A Division of The McGraw-Hill Companies

HISTORY AND THE INTERNET: A GUIDE
Published by McGraw-Hill, an imprint of the McGraw-Hill
Companies, Inc., 1221 Avenue of the Americas, New York, NY
10020. Copyright © 2002 by The McGraw-Hill Companies, Inc. All
rights reserved. No part of this publication may be reproduced or
distributed in any form or by any means, or stored in a database
or retrieval system, without the prior written consent of The
McGraw-Hill Companies, Inc., including, but not limited to, in any
network of other electronic storage or transmission, or broadcast
for distance learning.
Some ancillaries, including electronic and print components, may
not be available to customers outside the United States.

This book is printed on acid-free paper.

1 2 3 4 5 6 7 8 9 0   QWF/QWF   0 9 8 7 6 5 4 3 2 1

ISBN 0-07-251456-6

Publisher: *Thalia Dorwick*
Sponsoring editor: *Lyn Uhl*
Editorial assistant: *Kate Mullin*
Marketing manager: *Janise Fry*
Project manager: *Christina Thornton-Villagomez*
Production supervisor: *Carol Bielski*
Freelance design coordinator: *Mary Kazak*
Media Producer: *Sean Crowley*
Cover desiger: *Andrew Curtis*
Cover images: *© Photo Disc/© Image Book*
Interior design: *CRC*
Typeface: *12/13 Helvetica*
Compositor: *H&S Graphics Inc.*
Printer: *Quebecor World/Fairfield*

Library of Congress Control Number: 2001097385

www.mhhe.com

TABLE OF CONTENTS

INTRODUCTION

Students and teachers need to take the Internet and new instructional technologies seriously as potentially valuable and exciting tools for the study and teaching of history. We know the adoption of new technologies in the past such as the camera, railroads, the telegraph, the telephone, the automobile, the radio, motion pictures, television, film strips, the transistor, the VCR, and the personal computer have not always lived up to their expected or promised potential. The only way we can play a role in how e-mail; Web sites; online library catalogs, archival inventories, and primary sources; and CD-ROM's will be used in our classrooms, college dormitories, homes, businesses, and apartments will be if we investigate and experiment with them.

From the time we are children, we all learn that the record of the human past is a complicated tale involving the tangled Web of interactions among individuals, groups, regions, generations, nations, races, classes, sexes, ethnicities, cultures, and religions. The only way to capture even a partial understanding of the complex warp and woof of the human social fabric is to integrate a wide diversity of source materials that reflect the metaphorical dance of life in all its contradictions. Traditionally, historians and most scholars in the humanities and the social sciences have tried to make sense of the past by focusing their attention on written records, knowing that oral traditions, sounds, images, and artifacts can often be difficult if not impossible to find, assess, and synthesize as part of the human record. With the emergence of computer technology, digitization, scanners, and the ability to communicate almost instantaneously across the globe in the last few decades, we now have the possibility of a truly multidimensional way of creating historical interpretations that brings the past alive.

The time has come for historians to join with other humanists, social scientists, and scientists in making the effort to bring this possibility to light and practice. Every term as we begin courses anew, we discover that students have leaped ahead of teachers in using computer technology, e-mail, and surfing the Net to thrive in our modern, fast-paced society. If historians as teachers do not make the effort to join students in using these new means to help them in understanding the significance of history as a way of thinking, seeing, listening, and envisioning the past and present, we may wake up to a future that emerges as a dystopian nightmare rather than a utopian vision. Already, students perceive such new technologies as neither good nor bad, right or wrong, progressive or regressive—no Luddites here. Just as earlier generations learned to bring telephones, movies, radio shows, the television, the VCR, and the personal computer into their lives, we must learn to combine the best of the traditional ways of history with the best of the new ways of making history.

This guide is intended to provide both teachers and students with some of the knowledge about how we can make this transition to using a new set of tools to help us as craft workers laboring in the fields of human history. After providing an overview of the history of the Internet, the work centers on how to use an Internet browser and explore the World Wide Web as a form of hypertext and interactive historical learning. Web sites can function as online archives, while e-mail can promote multiple ways of communicating among students, between students and teachers, and among teachers and scholars. Search engines can help us to locate useful historical sources in the vast storehouse of the Internet, yet we must be thoughtful in evaluating the materials we find. People at all kinds of colleges and universities can now begin to access documents, texts, sights, and sounds that only a few years ago scholars at the best-funded research universities did not have available. Class assignments, research papers, presentations, and Web sites mean that control of publishing has in part been taken out of the hands of publishers and placed into the hands of individuals willing to take the initiative and use new means to collect, store, analyze, and distribute information that becomes knowledge through application of historical methods.

For the first time in human memory, we have the possibility of creating multimedia history that can spark a popular renaissance of historical thinking. Web sites, e-mail networks, and CD-ROMs, can bring together students, enthusiasts, teachers, scholars, and professional colleagues so that history need no longer be constrained by limited time, energy, and resources. As you explore the methods discussed here, please let the author know your thoughts, criticisms, and suggestions at preagan@tntech.edu.

ACKNOWLEDGMENTS

In the course of researching and writing this work, I have once again rediscovered the joy of working with talented, generous, and cooperative people. Don Mabry, Lynn Nelson, and Roy Rosenzweig engaged in thoughtful correspondence that gave me pause in thinking the project through. Peter Felten introduced me to the New Media Classroom project and acted as a solid sounding board for some ideas, while organizers and participants in the Blues, Bluegrass, and Blue Suede Shoes workshop at the Center for Teaching, Vanderbilt University kindly listened and offered many good Ideas. Chad Berry and Alice Carls graciously gave time, comments, and suggestions. Thanks to Ballard Campbell, Bob Cherny, Kris Lindenmeyer, and Michael Pierce of H-SHGAPE for giving me the opportunity to learn what creating a community can be. All of my colleagues in the Department of History at Tennessee Technological University continue to listen attentively to my thoughts about computers, gophers, Webs, and the Net more than anyone could hope for while providing encouragement and sometimes healthy skepticism along the way. Editors Lyn Uhl and Kate Mullin at McGraw-Hill committed to expansion of the original proposal, listened to the author's ideas, and gave positive feedback. Each knew exactly when to recruit, cajole, beg, prod, push, and encourage a busy author and new father. Reilly West Reagan gave unsparingly of her time, energy, respect, and love even though it was our first year as new parents. In hope that the subject matter may one day inspire, I dedicate this work to our son Daniel Patrick Joseph whose entry into the world in time for the new millennium suggests that the next generation may truly go where "no one has gone before."

ACKNOWLEDGMENTS

1. A BRIEF HISTORY OF THE INTERNET

What Is the Internet: When and How Did It Emerge?

Immediately following the end of World War II in 1945, few people had access to computers. During the early years of the Cold War, the federal government purchased and used most computers made in the United States for defense-related functions. The **Electronic Numerical Integrator and Calculator (ENIAC)** developed at the University of Pennsylvania included eighteen thousand vacuum tubes that took up an entire room. These early computers lacked the power, memory, and storage room possible with modern-day desktop and laptop computers found in every walk of life including college campuses, business offices, and government agencies. No one had yet considered the possibility of linking computers together into small networks, let alone a national or global system such as the **Internet** we take for granted today. Only a very small number of huge machines were connected with other computers over a standard telephone line that could transfer data only at very slow rates. The costs of operating such links proved more expensive than any potential benefits.

Today the Internet joins tens of millions of laptops, personal computers (PCs), work stations, and older main frame computers in a world wide network with the ability to perform multiple tasks at once very rapidly and at low cost using not only text but also images and sounds. Soon millions of wireless and cellular telephones, **personal digital assistants (PDAs)**, and as yet undreamed of **multimedia** devices will bring the Internet into classrooms, libraries, laboratories, offices, businesses, and homes.

The Internet began as a major Cold War defense research project. In 1962 the U.S. Air Force (USAF) asked the **RAND [Research and Development] Corporation**, a new think tank, to study how the USAF's command system could survive a nuclear attack. By 1964, **RAND** developed a plan for a decentralized military communications network that eventually would evolve into the Internet. Linking government defense computers into a system in which each station could receive and transmit information over many different routes would allow for continued communications in the event of nuclear war. If a nuclear attack destroyed one part of the system, the network could still transfer commands over the remaining circuits.

In 1969, the Department of Defense located in the Pentagon in Washington, D.C., inspired by the **RAND** proposal, created a modest, high-speed, four-computer network called **ARPANET (Advanced Research Projects Agency Network)**. By 1972, the network of computers for defense-related scientific research had grown more than nine-fold. Personal interactions of scientists changed the shape, history and purpose of the network. By 1974, scientists had transformed the system now called "the **Internet**" into an electronic mail service to exchange research, to speed up complex computations, and to provide a communication network to advance knowledge through what one historian of the Internet called "schmoozing" and "gossip." Everyday human interaction changed the Internet from a strategic instrument of the Cold War to a network that eased the flow of professional knowledge, national security information, and daily chatter – but not necessarily in that order.

Gradually, as the National Science Foundation replaced **ARPANET** as the supervisor of the **Internet** (a role that it turned over to private businesses in the mid-1990s), what began as a military-inspired government network for scientific research became a civilian system for education and later privatized systems for commercial development, information sharing, and mass entertainment. Between the 1970s and the 1990s, interaction between users created languages, programs, and tools that tens of millions of people in government, the professions, commerce, education, non-profit organizations, and households use every day in the form of **e-mail**, Web sites, **newsgroups**, and **listservs**.

In 1983, the **Internet** became what its name implies, a network of networks. The language, or protocol, called **TCP/IP (Transmission Control Protocol/Internet Protocol)** first developed in the seventies made transfer of information in electronic form possible from one point in the system to another. As **TCP/IP** became the uniform standard for the Internet, it enabled computers using different operating systems (Macintosh,

Unix, DOS, and Windows, and others) to communicate with one another.

In the 1990s, the Internet emerged as a high-speed, global system transporting text, graphics, sounds and **multimedia** materials across oceans and continents. From four computers in 1969, the Internet evolved into the **World Wide Web**.

From Text to Graphics: The Internet Goes Multimedia

Boosters and critics bestow many names on the modern-day Internet, especially the **World Wide Web (WWW** or **the Web)**, its most familiar modern form. "A software system running on the Internet." "A Web of knowledge." "A set of protocols." "A seamless world of information." "A universal information database." Or more dismissively, "just a bunch of links" and "trash."

In truth, the **World Wide Web** includes all the above. In 1989 Tim Berners-Lee, an English scientist, developed a design and the necessary software and protocols for the high-speed transmission and retrieval of information by the international community of physicists. Berners-Lee and colleagues at the **Conseil Européenne pour la Recherche Nucléaire [European Organization for Nuclear Research](CERN)** outside Geneva, Switzerland created a global system of computer communications allowing physicists to exchange data and research quickly and seamlessly to promote scientific cooperation across national boundaries.

Several protocols (languages or sets of standards) encouraged the flow of knowledge. One created a common language that enabled computers to talk to one another: **Hypertext Markup Language (HTML)**. A second, **Hypertext Transfer Protocol (HTTP)**, directed the traffic of **multimedia** information (text, graphics, sound, and video) between computers and across networks. A third established a standard for creating addresses or **Uniform Resource Locators (URL)** for computers sending and receiving information. Since **CERN** sought to promote academic exchange rather than commercial profit, it made its protocols and software public, enabling linked computers around the world to decipher and translate **HTML** and **HTTP**. Anybody could use this **multimedia** Web, but few anticipated just how quickly it would expand from a small community of scientists to today's vast numbers of government, education, commercial, and household users.

The Berners-Lee protocols transformed the **Internet**, allowing **CERN** scientists to export and import data as text, image, sound, and video files. Yet no one piece of integrated software existed with the capability of putting all this information in its different media forms onto a single computer screen. Text could be called up on one screen, images or graphics on another, sound on another, and video on still another. Before the Web would appeal to a larger, mass audience, software protocols and programs would have to become more user friendly.

By the early 1990s, scientists and programmers made significant advances in the software applications used to store and retrieve text information on the Web. Computer scientists at the University of Minnesota created the **"Gopher" system of text-based menus** named after the burrowing rodent which serves as the mascot of the University of Minnesota athletic teams. You could use a **Gopher** site to tunnel and dig for information using a series of hierarchically structured menus and submenus of data in text form. Every menu item was "hot," meaning that a click of the computer mouse over the menu link item took you to an information base or to a submenu with more choices for you to click. As a way of organizing and accessing large amounts of information, **Gopher** menus pioneered as a breakthrough making broad use of the **Internet** a real possibility. By today's standards, **Internet** surfers consider **Gopher** sites dinosaurs since they did not allow for accessing graphical images, sounds, or video. The hierarchical organization of the text-based **Gopher** menu system did not allow for the nonlinear linking of **hypertext**.

In 1993, development of the first practical **graphical user interface (GUI), soon known as a Web browser**, called **Mosaic** at the National Center for Supercomputing Applications (NCSA) at the University of Illinois dramatically transformed the organization and potential uses of the **Internet**. Very quickly alternate browsers emerged as competitors to **Mosaic** including the most popular and widely used software. **Microsoft Internet Explorer, Netscape Navigator**, or the **Opera** Web browsers gave the **World Wide Web** the face we know today, making it possible to present information in all its **multimedia** forms on a single screen. Web browser software translates **HTML**, the *lingua franca* or universal language of the WWW into text, images and sound, making it possible for you to access, read and make links between Web pages. A Web page is one or more screens of information which you see as text and/or images formatted in **Hypertext Markup Language or HTML**.

Internet Web **browsers** empower computer newcomers, called "newbies," unable to tell the difference between Hypertext Markup Language, SGML, or Javascript coding to view a Web page just as an experienced computer programmer might -- with the click of a mouse. **Browser** software allows you to actively use **e-mail**, visit Web sites, download files, subscribe to **listservs**, participate in **newsgroups** and employ other **Internet** tools which we will define and discuss later.

Mosaic, Microsoft Internet Explorer, Netscape Navigator, and the **Opera** browsers transformed the Web, turning it into an everyday tool that invited participation by the sheer ease of navigation. The creators of these browsers imported **GUIs (Graphical User Interfaces)** to the Web. For years, **GUIs** had been a staple of Macintosh computers, soon followed by personal computers with the Microsoft Windows operating systems. We recognize **GUIs** as icons, scroll bars, pull-down menus and dialog boxes, all activated by moving the Mouse pointer (the cursor) and clicking on the computer mouse. With **browser** software, these clicks can take you on a Web trip to sites around the world.

What we click on a Web page, using a Web **browser**, are icons, images or text (typically underlined and in color, usually blue). We drag the cursor on the computer mouse to "hot" text or graphics, and then click onto another screen. "Hot" means "linked" in computer terminology. We know that a Web image or words are hot when the dragged mouse cursor turns into a hand.

Knowledge as Hypertext: Text, Images, and Sound

Hot text is **hypertext**. Hot links are **hyperlinks**. Simply defined, **hypertext** is non-sequential, linked knowledge. **Hypermedia** is **hypertext** and non-sequential links of text, images, and sound. **Hypertext** and **hypermedia** have major implications for how we learn and organize knowledge. Typically, historians arrange knowledge into linear—that is, chronological—narratives. **Hypertext** and **hypermedia** encourage the organization of related knowledge in many different directions, not linear but connected like a spider's web.

A BRIEF HISTORY OF THE INTERNET

1962 – U.S. Air Force commissions **RAND Corporation** to develop a decentralized computer communications network that could survive a nuclear attack.

1969 – Pentagon develops **ARPANET**, a RAND-inspired, four-computer network for defense-related research.

1974 – A much-expanded ARPANET is now called the **Internet**. Participating scientists transform the Internet, creating e-mail to "schmooze," "gossip," and exchange research.

1983 – The Internet becomes a network of networks, made possible by a protocol called **TCP/IP (Transmission Control Protocol/Internet Protocol)** enabling computers using different operating systems (Macintosh, Unix, DOS, Windows) to communicate with one another.

1989 – English scientist Tim Berners-Lee develops software and protocols for the **World Wide Web**, making possible the high-speed transmission and retrieval of information by an international community of physicists.

1993 – **Mosaic** develops a user-friendly, mouse-driven graphical user interface or browser. On a single computer screen, information can now be organized and accessed in all of its multimedia forms. As a result, the Internet expands from a small community of scientists to today's vast popular, commercial, educational, non-profit, and government use.

1993 – Volunteer editors in various academic disciplines begin creating a worldwide system of virtual library sites (WWW-VL) maintained by scholarly experts.

1995 – Java programming language allows for animation and interactivity between computers using different operating systems.

1995 – National Science Foundation gives up control of the Internet backbone leading to privatization and commercialization of the Internet.

A BRIEF HISTORY OF THE INTERNET, continued

1995 – The Internet delivers more e-mail than the post office does letters.

2001 – Web sites become so numerous that new domain names must be developed.

In the fast moving history of the **World Wide Web**, **Mosaic** quickly became another relic of computer history. Several programmers left **Mosaic**, creating the **Netscape Navigator** Communications Corporation which developed the powerful, multitask browser, **Netscape Navigator**, setting the standard for the industry in the mid-nineties. Later, **Netscape Navigator** became part of America On Line, a major **internet** service provider for millions of people. Today, most Web surfers use the **Microsoft Internet Explorer**, Netscape Navigator, or the **Opera** browser, although other companies continue to make competing browser software. The latest generation of browser software not only makes it easier to receive data, but also comes with editing programs to create Web pages complete with text, hot links, graphics, sounds, forms, and other interactive features without having to know anything about how to program HTML. Widespread distribution and use of these browsers, oftentimes downloaded for free off the **Internet**, creates a potential for democratizing the Web, bringing the power of a worldwide system of information exchange to anyone with access to a linked computer.

Connecting to the Net: Modems, T-1/T-3 lines, and ISDN, Cable Modem, and DSL

Not everyone has access to a computer, let alone one wired to the Web. Some people and institutions have better, faster access than others. Access to the **Internet** depends on such factors as speed, convenience, cost, and politics. This guide will mainly discuss speed and convenience, but money and power sometimes determine how well connected you are, including your wired connection to the **Internet**. Rapid changes in computer software and hardware and dramatic declines in costs lower the price of admission to the Web, making **Internet** access more affordable for masses of users.

Many Web surfers use a low-cost **modem** with a dial-up connection to transmit signals over telephone lines, operating at speeds of 2,400 to 56,600 bits per second. As fast as that sounds, it's slow compared to a **T-1 line** (1.5 million bits per second or bps) or a **T-3 line** (45 million bps). **Modems** are relatively inexpensive and can tap into an ordinary phone line coming into your home, apartment, or dorm room. High speed **T-1** and **T-3** lines establish direct point-to-point connections into the trunk of the telephone system, generally only affordable to big corporations, universities, some government agencies, and **Internet service providers**. Like most things in this world, you get what you pay for. You notice the speed difference between a **modem** on a home computer and a **T-1** or **T-3** line on a college or business network when linking to a Web page. Increasingly, access to **Integrated Services Digital Network (ISDL)** with speeds of 16-64,000 bps), **cable modem** (with speeds of about one million bps), and **Digital Subscriber Line (DSL)** with various speeds up to 1.5 million bps equivalent to a **T-1** line) connections through a local, urban, or national **Internet Service Provider (ISP)** provide affordable compromises with faster speeds than dial-up **modems** and significantly lower costs than **T-1** and **T-3** lines.

Other factors such as the power of your computer, the speed of the **server** computer that holds the Web page you want to access, the size of the Web information you want to import, the volume of traffic on the **Internet**, and the online service (e.g. America On Line) or college network that is your **Internet Service Provider**. Given the rapid turnover in computer technology in this age of immediate gratification, our definition of quick changes rapidly. A few years ago, two-day and overnight mail via FedEx, the U.S. post office, and other private delivery services was considered fast.

Today, **e-mail** users derisively call the U.S. Postal Service "**snail mail**." When a Web page does not appear on a screen within seconds of a mouse click, most computer users become impatient. People with different kinds of **Internet** access experiencing "traffic jams" refer to the "World Wide Wait." Development of the second and third generation **Internet** and expansion of broadband capabilities through fiber optic cables over time will allow faster surfing and more widespread use of

multimedia materials such as animated and full-color images, sounds, music, and audiovisual film recordings. With some historical perspective, we can appreciate just how far and fast we have moved from the origins of the **Internet** just three decades ago.

Summary of Internet History

In 1995, the **Internet** delivered more **e-mail** than the U.S. Postal Service did letters. That's a staggering statistic, testimony to the centrality and remarkable growth of the **Internet**. Researchers at the Pew Internet & American Life Project discovered that by the end of the year 2000, 104 million Americans had access to the **Internet**. Tens of millions more people across the globe were getting hooked up to this international computer system. One observer characterized the "**Internet** as a city struggling to be built," a social creation evolving into a system meeting user needs through **e-mail**, the **World Wide Web**, **listservs**, **newsgroups**, remote logins through **Telnet**, and movement of files through **FTP (File Transfer Protocol)**. With its phenomenal expansion, the **Internet** created a whole new vocabulary: **e-mail**, surfing the Net, **Telnet**, and **FTP** that will be explained in coming chapters and in a **Glossary** in the **Appendix**.

Computers and their linking via the **Internet** expand the power of texts—the printed word—as well as images and sounds by their ability to store and process information in the form of binary digits (bits). Filtered through users' brains, information can be transformed into research and knowledge. Floppy, **ZIP**, and **CD-ROM** disks make that knowledge portable. Typically a **CD-ROM** can hold 650 megabytes, or the equivalent of—perish the thought—500 history textbooks. While that's impressive, it pales before the power of the **Internet,** which can store and transmit over long distances infinitely more knowledge in **digital** form. Once received, a computer can take that **digital** information and transform it into a Shakespeare sonnet, a Monet still-life, a Billie Holiday blues song, any one of thousands of electronic books or absolute, utter trash. As pioneers of the computer revolution used to say, "Garbage In, Garbage Out" (**GIGO**). The **Internet** can become what we make it, a powerful tool for creating and sharing knowledge or promoting mediocrity through moving disconnected bytes and bits; for spreading rumor and false knowledge or gaining access to rich primary sources and electronic texts via online library catalogs and historical archives. Most importantly, the **Internet** allows human beings to use computer technology to interact with one another, learn about the past, and share information and knowledge across the globe.

2. BROWSER BASICS FOR SURFING THE NET

Using Your Browser: The Basics

Web **browsers** provide a way for you as an **Internet** user to access resources available on millions of Web sites. Once installed onto a computer with an **Internet** connection, browser software can be started by clicking on an icon, a symbol representing a shortcut to the software program, most commonly **Microsoft Internet Explorer**, **Netscape Navigator**, or the **Opera** browser. The screen that opens on the Windows or Macintosh computers at your college probably already has a series of graphic symbols for software applications and accessories, including an icon for the **Internet** browser. Using the mouse, move the flashing cursor to the browser icon, click, and in seconds, as the browser software on your computer speaks to another computer nearby, across the country, or on the other side of the world, you move to a **home page** of a Web site embedded in a screen with menus, buttons, scrollbars and still more icons. Welcome to the **World Wide Web**.

Be adventurous. Think of "surfing the Net" as a game allowing you to explore a new world of information. Move your mouse cursor to the pull down menus at the top of your browser window (e.g. File, Edit, View, **Favorites**, Tools, and Help on **Microsoft Internet Explorer**; File, Edit, View, Search, Go, Bookmarks, Task, and Help on **Netscape Navigator**; or File, Edit, View, Navigation, Bookmarks, E-Mail, Messaging, News, Window, and Help on the **Opera** browser). See what is on each menu, and then each sub-menu. The easiest way to learn any new software program is to start at the top left of the menu, then work your way down each choice in a column, then over each column from left to right. Don't be afraid to click on an item. Your **browser** won't crash. If you are new to the Web (a "**newbie**"), go first to the Help menu for easy point and click lessons about how to use the **browser**. Last but not least, don't forget the buttons. As you move your mouse cursor across a button, a small box appears describing the button's function. A graphical Web **browser** can be a powerful tool opening up Web sites from around the globe. Like everything else, you learn by using—start with the **home page** that your **browser** opens to—then start exploring. As you become more familiar with the working of the **browser**, spend a set amount of time each day learning one or two new uses for the **browser**. Trying to learn all the operations of the software in one sitting may lead to frustration; however, learning only what you need to one thing at a time builds on your expanding **Internet** skills.

A **home page** represents the front door or top level to a Web site. The first page may be the only one or the first of hundreds inside the site. You can set up, or configure, your **browser** to open to any **home page** of your choice. Typically, at your campus, the **browser** goes to your college or university Web site, where you will undoubtedly find links to other pages that will get you past the front door: academic departments, programs of study, financial aid, the library, the records office, admissions, student organizations, institutional rules, and local news and events are some of the information you can find here. Most Web sites include **hypertext** links (usually blue and underlined), graphics, photographs, and special effects such as sound files and streaming video. Whenever you move the cursor and it turns into a hand, you can click the mouse on that link to connect to another page.

If you look at the top (sometimes at the bottom) of your **browser** screen, you will note a small rectangular box with a string of letters probably beginning with http://www. **Microsoft Internet Explorer** identifies the box as the "Address"; **Netscape Navigator** as the "Location," and the **Opera** browsers calls it the "Address bar." Every **home page** and its associated Web pages (inside the site) have an address, what we previously identified in Chapter One as a **Uniform Resource Locator (URL)**.

Without a logical address system, navigation of the Web would be next to impossible, akin to a postman delivering mail to anonymous individuals in a city with no street names, no house and apartment numbers, and no ZIP codes. The agreed-upon language, or protocol, for **URL**s lists Web site locations much like an address which consists of a combination of number, street, apartment, city, and ZIP codes.

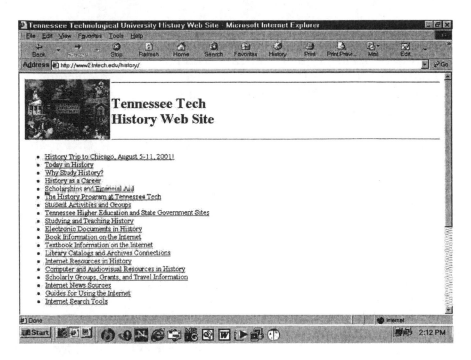

Reprinted with permission.

There are accepted conventions for **URL** names. Take for example the **home page** of the **Tennessee Tech History Web Site**, a guide to online resources in history (http://www2.tntech.edu/history/). The first part of the **URL** before the colon explains the means of **Internet** access, in this case **hypertext transfer protocol** (**http**). Alternatively, if this prefix read "file" or "**ftp**" (**file transfer protocol**) you would not access the Web, but rather a different **Internet** feature. The "www" in the **URL** specifies the resource, in this case the **World Wide Web**.

A computer **server** at Tennessee Technological University houses this Web site, as indicated by its **domain** name (tntech.edu). Any host computer on the **Internet** can be a **domain**. Three-letter designations, such as "**edu**" for education, "**gov**" for government, and "**com**" for commercial, indicate what kind of institution, organization or enterprise operates the host computer. You can find a fuller list and explanation of **domain** designations in Chapter Five, under the section **Electronic Mail**.

13

The names between slashes represent directories. The first, "history," is the name of an **Internet** site sponsored by the Department of History at Tennessee Tech and maintained by Tennessee Technological University, a guide for online history resources whose address we've been unraveling for the past several paragraphs.

So how do we get there? One way involves typing the **URL** in the Address or Location box, and then pressing the Enter key. You can also go to the menu on the top of the **browser** screen. Click File, then scroll down to a choice that, depending on your **browser**, reads "Open" or "Open Page." Click and a dialog box appears. Type the **URL** in the appropriate box, then—noting that sometimes these addresses can be sensitive to case, spacing and precise punctuation—press the Enter key or click "OK" (Microsoft **Internet** Explorer),"Open Page" (**Netscape Navigator**), or the curved arrow button (**Opera** browser).

You are now on the Tennessee Tech History Web Site. Move the mouse pointer to and click any of the **hypertext** hot links, for example, "Internet Resources in History." You are now moving from the TTU History **home page**, going through the door as it were and inside to the "Internet Resources in History" Web page. Look at the **URL** address or location box at the top of your screen. Note the new **URL** (http://www2.tntech.edu/history/resources.html). The new address signifies a directory called "resources," the one that we clicked after pointing the mouse to the link on the **home page** entitled "Internet Resources in History."

Sometimes to know where we are, it's important to know where we've been. With your mouse, move the cursor to the box in the **URL** address or location window. Highlight and then delete "resources.html" from the address. Press Enter and almost instantaneously you are back on the TTU History **home page**. You are now at the **home page** of the Tennessee Tech History Web Site.

MAKING SENSE OF A WEB ADDRESS

We started with the URL (Web address) of the Tennessee Tech History Web Site. The first part of the URL before the colon explains the means of Internet access, in this case hypertext transfer protocol (http). The www that follows indicates the Internet resource, in this case the World Wide Web.

http://www2.tntech.edu/history/

When we click the hot link "Internet Resources in History," note how the URL changes:

http://www.tntech.edu/history/<u>resources.html</u>

When we delete "resources.html" from the URL, we go back to a sub-directory, "history," an Internet project sponsored by the Department of History at Tennessee Technological University. Note that the URL now ends with "history/."

http://www2.tntech.edu/history/<u>resources.html</u>

If we delete "history/resources.html" from the URL, we go back to the domain, "tntech.edu." A domain is the host computer, in this instance, Tennessee Technological University. Three-letter designations such as "edu" (education), "org" (organization), "com" (commercial) or "gov" (government) indicate what kind of institution is home to the host computer. Note that the URL now ends with "tntech.edu/."

http://www.tntech.edu/<u>history/resources.html</u>

In sum, the URL "http://www2.tntech.edu/history/resources.html" breaks down into these components:

http:// The means of access – Hypertext Markup Language
www The Internet feature – World Wide Web
tntech.edu Domain name – An educational (edu) institution
history First sub-directory – Tennessee Tech History Web Site
resources Second sub-directory – Internet Resources in History page
html Program language – Hypertext Markup Language

It sounds like the total confusion of the old Abbott and Costello comedy routine about "who's on first." But despite the initial blur of protocols, **domains**, directories, sub-directories and files, upon closer study these **URL** naming schemes follow a logical form of organization and naming. An even easier way to navigate from one page to any other you visited can be done by simply pointing and clicking the "Back" and "Forward" buttons on your **browser**. If we reversed our steps from the Tennessee Tech History gateway, we would click back, moving to "resources.html" bringing us back to the "Internet Resources in History" page.

Feeling lost? We can build a shortcut to any of these Web destinations by creating a place-saver. If you like what you see on a Web page, look for the **Favorites** (Microsoft Internet Explorer) or the **Bookmarks** (**Netscape Navigator** and **Opera browser**) button or menu. Open, scroll down to, and click "Add to Favorites" (**Internet Explorer**), "Add Bookmark" (**Netscape Navigator**) or "Add current document here" (**Opera**). If you saved the Tennessee Tech History site, you will see "Tennessee Technological University History Web Site" listed next time you go to "Bookmarks" or "Favorites." Highlight the entry, click (or press Enter), and no matter where you are on the Web, you'll be transported back to the Tennessee Tech History Web Site.

By now, you probably notice something rather annoying. Each **browser** has a different vocabulary for simple commands. Rather than standardizing language, they each try to put their own commercial signature on their software. So a **Bookmark** on one **browser** becomes a **Favorite** or **Hotlist** on another. Use common sense if you find yourself on a computer with an unfamiliar **browser** with equally strange language. The basic commands on browsers stay pretty standard; only the names and icons are different. You don't have to be a rocket scientist to figure out that **Favorite** or Hotlist is a synonym for **Bookmark**. Similarly, a red light icon represents the same thing as a Stop sign (which you click when you want to stop the connection to a Web site that is excruciatingly slow to load onto your **browser**).

Making the Browser a Practical Utility

Once you get used to how your **browser** works, you will find navigation fast and simple. As we have seen, you can Bookmark sites, go Back and Forward, and from most any Web page, link to others. If you want, you can readily access a history of every site you visited over the past three weeks. On **Microsoft Internet Explorer**, click the History button on the menu which will present you with a list on the left side of sites you have visited. On **Netscape Navigator**, click Communicator or Tasks(depending on which version of Netscape you use), then Tools, then History. You open to a window listing the name, **URL** and date visited of every site. Scroll down to any site you wish to re-enter, click (or press Enter) and you are there. With the **Opera browser**, just click on the Back button until you reach the site you want.

Click the Search icons on your **browser**, and a page with links to **search engines** appears. You can use these sites to search for data stored on virtually every Web site in the world. (More about this in Chapter Six). If a Web site you are trying to visit loads onto your **browser** too slowly, click Refresh (Microsoft Internet Explorer) or Reload (**Netscape Navigator** and **Opera**) in the hope that you will get a better connection to the host computer. If (and I emphasize "if") all goes well, the page should load faster. If it doesn't, and your patience becomes thin, you might want to click the stop button to terminate the connection. Some people have become increasingly frustrated with the slow speed of the **Internet** as more users access the Net that they joke about how the **World Wide Web** has become the World Wide Wait. As the newer generations of the **Internet**, sometimes called **Internet 2** and **Internet 3**, come online, those with access to these networks at member research universities will find speeds increasingly getting faster as bandwidth becomes larger, allowing for "broadband" access through faster connections made possible by multiple **T-1** and **T-3** lines, **cable modems** and **DSL** connections.

By saving, you can capture every page and image you view, preserving it as a Web file. Click the File menu, then Save. A dialog box will instruct you to name the file and designate a floppy disk, **Zip disk**, or hard drive folder location where you wish to save the file. Using your **browser**, you can then view and open the site from your floppy disk, **Zip disk** or hard drive. Newer versions of **Microsoft Internet Explorer** enable users to retrieve whole Web sites, with their many layers of pages, and store them on a hard drive.

You can capture an image on a Web page by pointing and clicking your mouse (right click the image if you use a Windows platform; click and hold on a Macintosh platform). A dialog box will then appear. To view the image as a new page, click on "Open" (**Microsoft Internet Explorer**); File, then Open File/Page (**Netscape Navigator**); or File, then New, and type in the **URL** (**Opera**). The dialog box will also provide a menu option that will allow you to "Save Picture as" (Microsoft Internet Explorer), "Save Image as" (**Netscape Navigator**) or "Save Image" (**Opera**) on your hard drive, **Zip disk**, or floppy disk. More advanced versions of Microsoft Word, Word Perfect, and other word processing programs allow you to import these images into word processing documents.

You can shape the **browser** environment in many ways to fit your needs. To make pages load faster, you might want to suppress pictures, sounds, graphics and **Java** (a programming language that allows for animated graphics). Text-only makes for a much swifter connection. You can change colors, fonts, the page that your **browser** opens to, the icons on your toolbar, and much more. In turn, you can organize bookmarks into folders and sub-folders. The means by which you re-decorate and configure depends upon your **browser**. Go to the Help menu for the necessary instructions.

Adding to the Power of Your Browser

Your **browser** should be a work in progress. You can enhance its power as a **multimedia** tool by adding features, called Active X controls (**Microsoft Internet Explorer**) or **Plug-In's** (**Netscape Navigator** and **Opera**). Even using the latest versions of **browsers**, new Web pages use special files, sound, animation or movies that you may not be able to view. Do not worry, since a menu or button will invariably appear telling you that you need a **plug-in** or Active X control. The **browser** gives you the option of downloading the add-on. If you decide to download by hitting the button or hotlink, instructions will appear on your screen explaining how to do it. Once the download process finishes, the add-on becomes part of your **browser**. Some of the more popular **plug-in**'s are Apple **QuickTime** (movies), **Shockwave** (animation), Real Player (sound and video), and Real Juke Box (sound files, pre-recorded music from CDs, and music accessed and purchased from online sites).

There's still more power in your **browser**. Newer versions of Microsoft Internet Explorer and **Netscape Navigator** (1) provide authoring tools that make it easy to create Web pages, while all three major **browsers** allow you to (2) send and receive **e-mail**, (3) transfer files in text, sound, images and video by means of **FTP (File Transfer Protocol)**, (4) connect to libraries around the world via **telnet**, and (5) facilitate good talk on a variety of topics through **newsgroups** and chat room software add-ons. Some of these features will be discussed in future chapters; much of it changes too quickly to describe in detail. You can explore how to use the power of this software by going to the Help menu of your **browser** or to another medium—a good, old-fashioned book. Many excellent print manuals on any one of these topics are available in the computer section of your local bookstore, while others can be found through **Internet** search sites such as Alta Vista, Google, Northern Light, Yahoo, and other **search engines** which can be found at Search Engine Watch (http://www.searchenginewatch.com/).

3. KNOWLEDGE AS HYPERTEXT AND INTERACTIVE LEARNING

The Web as Hypertext

How do we organize and connect knowledge? In everyday life, many of us do it intuitively. Looking at a family photograph, smelling a flower, or seeing a police cruiser immediately triggers associations, emotions and memories. Our mind then creates trails of knowledge and experience that may take us in several different directions. Written or printed text usually appears in linear form as a progression of logical thoughts; however, human knowledge often gets organized in a non-linear arrangement that may or may not follow logical thought patterns. In contemporary culture, we often follow ideas, images, and sounds based on associations that can be organized as **hypertext**, a series of links allowing for multiple ways of making sense of the material.

The structure of the **Internet** and the **World Wide Web** encourages multiple paths of association made possible and accessible through the use of **hypertext**. In a 1945 essay entitled "As We May Think," presidential science advisor Vannevar Bush anticipated the **Internet** by envisioning a thinking machine that would function a lot like human memory. It would create networks or webs of association.

In the 1960s, T.H. Nelson gave this way of thinking a name: **hypertext**—and a home: the computer. By **hypertext**, he wrote:

> I mean non-sequential writing—text that branches and allows choices to the reader, best read at an interactive screen. As popularly conceived, this is a series of text chunks connected by links that offer readers different pathways.

In essence, Nelson saw the computer as Vannevar Bush's thinking machine. Text on a computer screen could be linked to text on another screen, the links following many different routes. Together, these **hyperlinks** could bring context, breadth and interaction to our knowledge while pushing it down many different paths. Let's look at an example on the **World Wide Web**.

Go to **The Victorian Web**

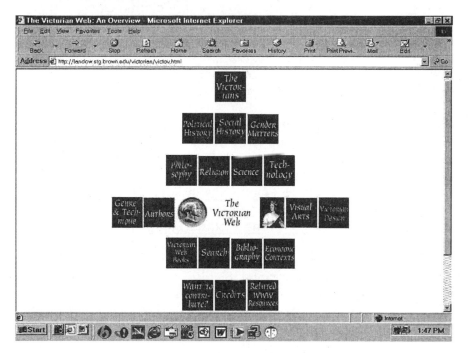

Reprinted with permission.

The Victorian Web (http://www.victorianweb.org/) is an excellent example of a page that creates interdisciplinary links across multiple disciplines. The Victorian age in Britain takes its name from and roughly corresponds to the sixty-four year reign (1837-1901) of Queen Victoria. During this period, the British empire expanded internationally, while domestically major developments occurred in the arts, literature, science, architecture, economics, politics, technology and what came to be called Victorian morality. Using threads from these various subject areas, a student entering the Victorian Web site can weave a **multimedia** interpretation that re-creates the fabric and texture of the Victorian age.

Note how the **home page** is organized. The centerpiece consists of a reproduction of a coin with an image of Queen Victoria and her husband Prince Albert alongside a painting of the Queen. Small, rectangular boxes surround these images with the following subject headings: <u>The Victorians</u>, <u>Political History</u>, <u>Social History</u>,

Gender Matters, Philosophy, Religion, Science, Technology, Genre & Technique, Authors, Visual Arts, Victorian Design, Victorian Web Books, Search, Bibliography, Economic Contexts, Want to Contribute?, Credits, and Related WWW Resources. Each box represents a hot link that will take you to more detailed resources in the topic. A click of the mouse will take you to a related Web page with a sub-menu.

Click Authors, then Charles Dickens, and you are transported to a screen with a picture of a pensive Charles Dickens connected by a theme map to categories such as Biography, Works, Economic Contexts, Political History, Social History, Religion, Science, Genre & Mode, Literary Relations, Visual Arts, Themes, Characterization, Imagery, Narrative, Bibliography, and a button to return to the **home page** of The Victorian Web. The page encourages you to put Dickens' work into an interdisciplinary context and to explore an incredible variety of **hypertext** connections including biography, history, culture, genre, images, and further references. You decide what roads to travel, how to put Dickens' novels in context, and how to build a chain of links that expands your and our understanding of Dickens.

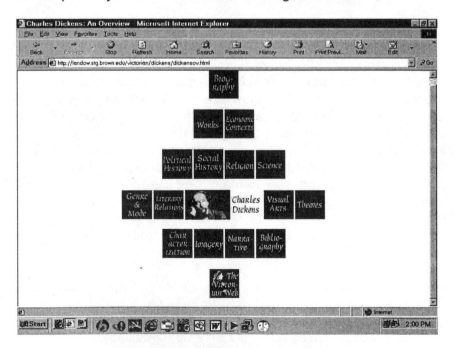

Reprinted with permission.

From the <u>Charles Dickens</u> map, go to <u>Economic Contexts</u> and a screen will appear on your monitor with links to essays on the economic conditions of Victorian capitalism, how publishers paid authors in Dickens' time, and the installments payments that Dickens received for his literary works.

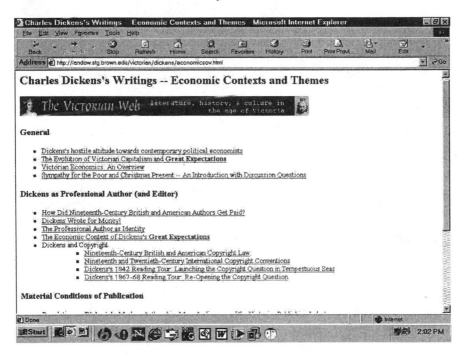

Reprinted with permission.

Go back to the <u>Charles Dickens</u> map and click on <u>Social History</u>. You will see a menu with the following choices:

<u>The Social Context of Dickens' Novels</u>

<u>The Class Significance of "The Tugges at Ramgate"</u>

<u>Child Labor</u>

<u>Dickens and Social Class</u>

<u>Economic Contexts</u>

<u>The Evolution of Victorian Capitalism and Great Expectations</u>

Melodrama as Theatricalized Dissent in Oliver Twist

Charles Dickens and Two Kinds of Punch

Dickens "the man who invented Christmas"

See also

Charles Dickens and Great Expectations – Social and Political Contents

Themes in Little Dorrit

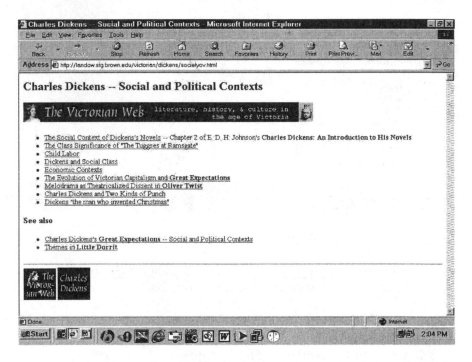

Reprinted with permission.

From this menu, you can explore all sorts of social themes, novels and even Dickens' own experience as a twelve-year old child laborer.

All these links enable you to investigate Victorianism in depth. You not only look at the period from many perspectives, but you become an active historian. You decide how to connect this information in ways that build your understanding of the interaction between historical actors, themes, causes and effects.

The Web as an Interactive Learning Space

The **Internet** can transform the intellectual geography of knowledge by creating a vast, constantly expanding learning space, with tremendous possibilities for interactive learning between students, teachers, scholars, and Web site editors. It builds on information accumulated by past generations, while in important ways changing our relationship to knowledge. With the potential to put computer users at the center of a Web of ever-expanding information, **Internet** sites can nourish active learning and empower student to both receive and construct knowledge while interacting through **hypertext** and **hyperlinks** with teachers and knowledgeable scholars.

Internet enthusiast Nicholas Negroponte, author of the best selling book *Being Digital*, argues that unlike television where "all the intelligence is at the point of transmission" and "little…at the point of reception," **digital** media (**WWW** and **CD-ROMs**) can turn consumers of information into producers of knowledge. TV is an electronic medium where producers construct input and, no matter how elegant or dismal the product, viewers do little more than passively receive it as output. All the creativity rests with those who control the transmission. On the Web, by contrast, it's much harder to be a couch potato. Students become practitioners of the historical method constructing interpretations based on primary and secondary sources researched and found under the direction of scholars who edit Web sites and guided by the knowledge and classroom experience of seasoned teachers. Historical study becomes truly an interactive learning experience bringing together students and teachers as researchers, writers, and historians learning how to use the historical method in a **multimedia** environment that everyone benefits from using.

As we see with the example of **The Victorian Web**, you can only put that site to effective use if you (1) research primary and secondary sources, (2) expand understanding by linking to other pages, and (3) build an historical interpretation based on the complicated patterns of historical and other disciplinary methods.

Reading of historical sources can be a passive experience. Interactive learning through the use of **hypertext** and **hyperlinks** brings students and teachers into an active learning mode. The resulting knowledge leads to the use of new technology to create a positive and personal interaction among historical sources, student, and teacher that allows for the building of sophisticated interpretations based on an understanding of historical context.

The **Internet** not only connects you to growing networks of **hyperlinks**, but through **e-mail**, and electronic and academic discussion groups to other students, professors, and professional and amateur practitioners in every intellectual discipline. It's a medium that promotes inquiry, collaboration, and cooperative learning.

4. HISTORY AND THE WORLD WIDE WEB

The Web as Historical Archives

Go to the **WWW-VL [Virtual Library] History Central Catalogue** (http://www.ku.edu/history/VL/), a Web sited maintained by Lynn Nelson at the University of Kansas. At first glance, the site opens to a page of worldwide links that may seem overwhelming. Put in perspective, however, those hundreds of links prove less daunting when compared to the archives of major public or university libraries such as the Library of Congress, public libraries in New York, Boston, and Chicago and academic research libraries such as the University of California at Berkeley, Harvard University, the University of Michigan, and the University of Virginia.

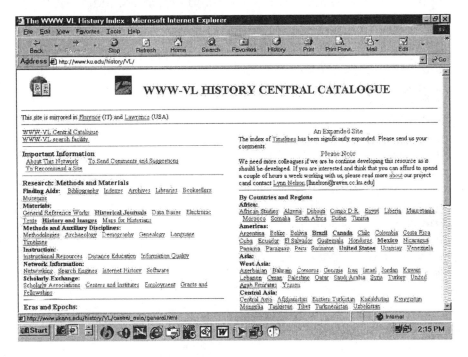

Reprinted with permission.

But when compared to most college collections, the History Central links can put students in touch with archives of primary documents and galleries of images well beyond the capacity of the average campus library. What's more, these links are expanding

27

at breathtaking speed as more and more archives are put on line. As a result it often takes several minutes for your **browser** to load the site when using a dialup **modem** connection. Entering the Virtual Library rewards the wait, bringing a treasure trove of historical material to your fingertips. University of Kansas historian Lynn Nelson and other historians have labored for years to collect the best history-related sites on the **Internet**, using this site as the focal point for a worldwide center resulting in the WWW Virtual Library in History. Part of the global Virtual Library system (WWW-VL) begun in 1993, the site harnesses the efforts of forty unfunded, volunteer editors, each an expert scholar in the specific field of study, who collect and list the best sources in that discipline at a central Web site. Click on the "Russia" link under "Europe" to find primary and secondary sources chronicling the history of Russia in the pre-Kiev period, relating the shift from Imperial Russia to the Soviet Union and leading to the modern Russian Federation in the post-Cold War period.

Don Mabry of Mississippi State University operates the **Historical Text Archive** (http://historicaltextarchive.com/), another comprehensive history site that gathers primary sources such as documents and images gleaned from Mabry's involvement with **e-mail**, **FTP**, and computers since 1989. The site includes **e-mail** comments from students of history ranging from undergraduate students to research scholars who have written articles and books on a professional basis. What began as a relatively small project at Mississippi State has become a huge project located on its own computer **server** with contributions from people all over the world. It has become one of the major **Internet** archives in the field of history, revealing the possibilities of using the **Internet** to make historical research available to a wide array of students in both classroom and informal settings.

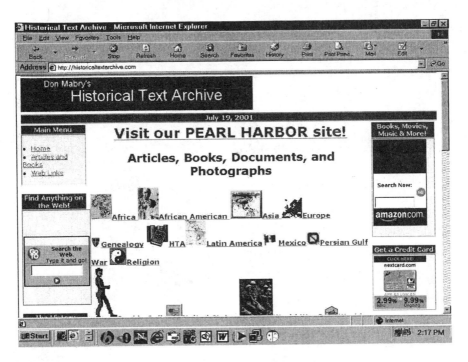

Reprinted with permission.

Some archive-rich libraries have started digitizing their repositories, with ambitious strategies to put them on the **Internet** as part of an emerging system of **digital** libraries. **American Memory: Historical Collections for the National Digital Library** (http://memory/loc.gov/) at the Library of Congress is one of the most successful and fastest growing such projects. By 2001, the American Memory Project offered over seven million images including text, audio, photographs and movies. As of June 2001 one hundred collections were already on the site ranging from revolutionary and constitutional documents to Civil War photographs to early motion pictures to Jackie Robinson breaking the color line in baseball to rich textual, photographic and audio archives from the Depression of the 1930s. Students and teachers can access these collections through an easy-to-use searchable database, making it possible not only to find material, but to organize and connect it across the many digital archives and galleries of the American Memory Project.

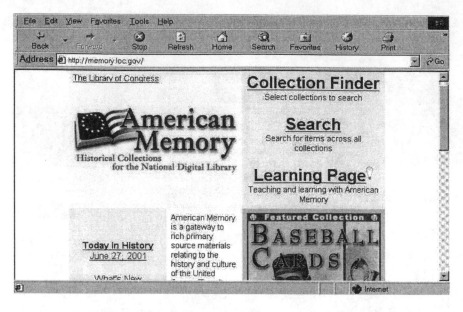

In addition to providing **Internet** surfers access to this portion of America's vast cultural legacy contained at the Library of Congress, the American Memory Project also includes the Today in History feature with historical facts, pictures, and documents about that day in history; a Learning Page (http://memory.loc.gov/ammem/ndlpedu/index.html) with activities, lessons, and resources for teachers and students; and the Collection Finder (http://memory.loc.gov/ammem/collections/ finder.html) that helps you to find text-based documents, maps, motion pictures, sound recordings, and **digital** materials in a range of formats (**jpeg, mpeg, MP3, QuickTime, RealPlayer, SGML, tiff,** and **wav file formats**).

Historical Inquiry on the Web

At the University of Virginia, Edward L. Ayers, Anne S. Rubin, William G. Thomas, III and a talented staff have created a huge but very focused **digital** archive called **Valley of the Shadow: Two Communities in the American Civil War** (http://jefferson.village.virginia.edu/vshadow2/) that encourages historical inquiry by inviting students to construct history from primary sources, much as professional historians do. An introduction to the site explains the scope and purpose of the project.

The Valley of the Shadow Project takes two adjoining communities on either side of the Mason-Dixon line, one Northern and one Southern, through the experience of the American Civil War. Its creators have brought together in a **hypermedia** archive thousands of sources for the period before, during and after the Civil War for Augusta County, Virginia, and Franklin County, Pennsylvania. Those sources include newspapers, letters, diaries, photographs, maps, church records, population census, agricultural census, and military records. Students can explore every dimension of the conflict and write their own histories, reconstructing the life stories of women, African Americans, farmers, politicians, soldiers, and families. Reflecting the emergence of the new social history of the last generation, this project allows students to delve into the origins, course, and consequences of the Civil War in a way that goes considerably beyond the traditional military focus on battles and campaigns and the political leadership of Abraham Lincoln and Jefferson Davis. Under the directed questioning of classroom teachers, students can investigate the history of the home front, the impact of economic mobilization, the role of rank and file soldiers, the history of women on both sides, and how the war affected the lives of Southern slaves and free blacks in the North. Unlike many history-related sites on the **Internet**, this one allows for real interaction between students and historical sources. The staff continues to add new materials and digitize sources that have been collected and cataloged earlier to give students a working example of how an historical archive constantly changes to incorporate new source materials, new questions, and new scholarship. In 2000, the project published the first of a projected three-disk **CD-ROM**, *The Eve of War* (http://www.wwnorton.com/vos/) (discussed in Chapter 8) containing primary sources from the prewar collection for individual use on Macintosh and Windows-based personal computers.

Archival sites like the Valley of the Shadow transform the relationship between students and history. For most students in a survey course, history is received knowledge from texts and lectures directed and controlled by the teacher as authority figure. When an instructor requires a research paper and/or asks you to interrogate primary sources and/or leads a probing discussion, history becomes inquiry, a kind of intellectual detective exercise. A well-designed and maintained Web site facilitates that inquiry in

31

ways that many textbooks cannot, while empowering the student to engage history as an active learner rather than a passive listener.

A good textbook does a lot of the work for you: shaping history into a meaningful narrative. That secondary text might provide you with an excellent base of factual information, but you do not necessarily have the skills of historical investigation or the access to primary sources necessary to question its interpretation. At the Valley of the Shadow, the creators provide a series of narratives that, much like a textbook, interpret the material for you. But there's a difference. They also present you with an archive that allows you to create your own narrative, and if so inclined, analyze, or deconstruct, theirs. If you are a novice historian, that's easier said than done. When you ask interpretive questions and then sift through the raw material in the Valley archive, for example writing a research paper, you are in fact doing what a professional historian does: constructing a narrative text out of primary sources.

It becomes more difficult for the historian to reassemble the past when print sources are scattered across the globe, sometimes badly preserved in dusty archives. That underscores the utility of a site like **The Labyrinth: Resources for Medieval Studies** (http://labyrinth.georgetown.edu/) which houses under a single **digital** roof primary sources, databases, electronic libraries, professional directories, online texts, syllabi, learning materials, **hypertext** links and its own **search engine**. Such a centralized, **digital** resource enables students and scholars to preserve, share and expand knowledge about medieval history. While sites like The Valley of the Shadow and The Labyrinth take advantage of the archival potential of the new medium of the **Internet**, some traditional archives such at the **Chicago Historical Society** (http://www.chicagohs.org/) integrate the best of the old with the most innovative of the new media to present primary sources, online exhibits, and special events to use the new technology to enhance the classic role of historical archives.

Let's look at one more Web page that gives its users tools to create historical meaning: **Nagasaki Journey** (http://www.exploratorium.edu/nagasaki/mainn.html). The site focuses on the dropping of an atomic bomb on the Japanese city of Nagasaki on August 9, 1945. You experience this by looking at astonishing photographs, followed by first and second person testimony by people of many different generations, viewpoints and nationalities (mainly Japanese and American), followed by a forum with participants from around the world on such topics as the atomic bomb, war and peace, and nuclear science. If you want, you could reverse the sequence, first exploring the forum or the first and second person testimony, then the photographs. The site literally bombards you with images and text: wrenching pictures, the recorded memories of survivors, testimony by Japanese and American soldiers, and reactions from generations born long after the war who could only experience Nagasaki second-hand. There is no overriding narrative to make sense of all this. In effect, the site begs the viewer to engage the material, to make links to related sites, to put the pieces together, and to interpret the event, its aftermath, and lessons. You are the historian.

The Web and Historical Simulation

The **hypertext** structure of the Web also allows for historical simulation. In other words, it can help you make a leap in place and time so that you are in the shoes of a historical character at a key turning point. Unlike computer games that depend on the programming skills and vision of the game designers, this kind of historical replay leads you through circumstances faced by real people at a time distant from and very different than the present. For example, the **Crisis at Fort Sumter** (http://www.tulane.edu/~latner/) site transports you to a virtual White House where you see a crisis unfolding through the eyes of President Abraham Lincoln and his cabinet in the late winter and early spring of 1861. Armed with actual documents from the period, you confront conflicting options, each choice leading to a different set of historical outcomes. What do you decide to do? As you face each situation, you have a choice of clicking any one of several links that would lead you down different trajectories. Were there alternative courses to the ones Lincoln selected in 1861? A mouse click does not have the anguish of a real-life presidential decision, but it can give you some sense of the possibilities and consequences tormenting a worried president at a major crossroad in U.S. history. Yet what makes such a simulation different from alternative history or historical fiction works is that you interact with documents and images from the time that place limitations on what you can do in a given situation, while helping you to understand that history is not predetermined but open to the contingent choices of human actors at a given point in time. This time, your choices reflect the possibilities and limits of a given historical situation rather than the wide-open alternate realities found in a game based on imagination.

Multimedia Sources on the Internet

Historical evidence comes in many forms: written and printed text, sketches, paintings, single, electronic images, sounds, film and news clips, motion pictures, and physical artifacts. The Web gives historical investigation a **multimedia** dimension, enabling users to examine archives of art, photographs, cartoons, lithographs, music, oral history, speeches and graphic reproductions of artifacts.

Students and faculty, for example, can explore the sounds, discography and history of jazz as well as the connections between Africa, the Caribbean and North America by exploring **multimedia** Web sites. Such a Web musical journey might begin with the Red Hot Jazz Archive, continuing with the Foundation Course in African Dance Drumming, and concluding with music by Bobby Sanabria.

The Red Hot Jazz Archive (http://www.redhotjazz.com/) is a comprehensive commercial Web site with discographies, links, page after page exploring historical themes, and one of the best jazz audio libraries on the **Internet**. With a **Real Player or audio plug-in** (which you can download for free at http://www.real.com/) or the **Windows Media Player** (also free to download at http://www.microsoft.com/ windows/windowsmedia/), you can listen to sounds as varied as Jelly Roll Morton's "Black Bottom Stomp," swing, boogie, and jazz-rock fusion.

The Foundation Course in African Dance Drumming (http://www.cnmat.berkeley.edu/~ladzekpo/Foundation.html) is an academic site housed at the University of California, Berkeley and constructed by C.K. Ladzepko, performer, composer, professor and director of the university's African Music Program. Using audio, video and text, the site guides users through the music and history of the Anglo-Ewe people of Ghana and parts of the sub-

Sahara. Listening to the West African drums suggests links to American jazz.

On an obviously commercial site, **Bobby Sanabria** (http://www.jazzcorner.com/sanabria/sanabriahome.html), this jazz musician promotes his tours and CDs while making connections between the African Diaspora, the Caribbean and North America.

The **National Museum of African Art** (http://www.nmafa.si.edu/) at the Smithsonian Institution gives visual context to the history of West Africa presenting many Web exhibitions, including one entitled, "In the Presence of Spirits: African Art from the National Museum of Ethnology, Lisbon." This online exhibit showcases African art from Angola, Mozambique and Guinea-Bissau ranging from dolls and stools to masks and power figures that have never been shown in the United States before now. Using the reach of the **Internet**, this kind of electronic show can bring the artifacts, paintings, and sculptures of museums directly to your computer monitor allowing you time to examine, appreciate, and revel in the artistic treasures of the world while studying cultural and historical themes.

At the **Art Museum Network** (http://www.amn.org/) site, you can locate and access online sites to museums all over the world, use a **search engine** to find over 50,000 online works of art, and find out about art collections, permanent exhibits, and special exhibits through an announcement network cosponsored by the Reuters news groups. While studying ancient Greece and Rome, the high Middle Ages, early modern Asia, pre-colonial Africa, and modern Latin America, you can use art history as a way to understand major cultural, intellectual, and religious changes over time. Depending upon the organization and design of each given site, you may need to download and install particular kinds of software such as Apple **QuickTime** or **Shockwave**. Many sites with these kinds of requirements place a button taking you to the download site to get the software necessary to fully utilize the site.

By providing such abundant imagery of art, photography and moving pictures, the Web encourages users to sharpen their skills of visual literacy. One does not, however, develop these skills automatically as a result of some kind of magical Web osmosis. Rather, with online museums and archives providing models of how to give meaning and historical context to images, more and more history professors are giving class assignments to collect, sort, curate and construct exhibits of visual evidence on a particular historical theme or period. Some professional organizations have begun creating online projects to identify, collect, digitize, and make publicly available archives of **digital** images for use by students and teachers. Network editors and staff members at **H-Net: Humanities and Social Sciences Online** (http://www2.h-net.msu.edu/) are discussing creation of a library of images for classroom use, while the Visible Knowledge Project: Learning/Technology/Inquiry (http://crossroads.georgetown.edu/vkp/) wants teachers to begin thinking about the importance of teaching visual literacy skills that can enhance student learning using images from the **Internet**.

Historical Discussion and Collaboration on the Internet

In sum, the Web allows you to explore history with lots of company. Scholars, students, amateur history buffs, government officials and agencies, universities, publishing houses, private firms, think tanks, partisans, and propagandists of many different stripes have built and continue to create a vast array of history sites. The entire set constitutes a kind of global archive. Some of these sites are excellent; others quite horrible. All of this raises a question: How do we evaluate history whether it's in printed or **digital** form? Through **e-mail**, **listservs** and sites dedicated to evaluating the quality of specific sites, the **Internet** creates communities that can be remarkably democratic where professionals and amateurs—teachers and students—can evaluate Web pages and discuss historical evidence, causation, interpretation, method and relevance. Being online with a professor may seem intimidating, admittedly sometimes it is, yet the flow of discussion can make the craft of history seem a lot less mysterious and help you refine your own skills to interpret the past. The Web can be a wonderful learning space for the exploration and practice of history from the search for primary sources, through the collection of texts, images, sounds, and artifacts, to the presentation of sophisticated historical interpretations that encourage cooperation and collaboration among students and between students and teachers.

5. E-MAIL AND DISCUSSION LISTS AS LEARNING TOOLS

Electronic Mail

The **Internet** allows people to interact with one another—it is a place for social interaction. **Electronic mail (e-mail)** helps individuals to communicate with each other through a two-way dialog. Using the **Internet**, **e-mail** lets you send, receive, respond to, store, print and forward messages, texts, reports, gossip, and, if you have the right software, graphical images, sound files, short audiovisual clips, Web pages, and entire Web sites. If everything works optimally, you can send **e-mail** almost instantaneously to one person or literally hundreds. To use **e-mail** you need an account, some basic software (often provided by your school, **Internet** provider, or as part of the **browser** software package) and a connection, either by **modem** to a dial-up commercial service (e.g. AOL, ATT WorldNet Service, CompuServe, EarthLink, MCI Mail, MSN, Prodigy, or any one of thousands of providers such as those included on The List: The Definitive ISP Buyer's Guide at http://thelist.internet.com) or directly to a client/**server** network like the one at your university or college.

E-mail can expand the classroom and re-shape the environment in which you learn. On one level, teachers become more accessible to students, in effect expanding office hours to twenty-four hours a day, seven days a week. Unlike using the telephone, you can **e-mail** a teacher at any time, day or night. Of course, your teacher may not be awake, let alone online to receive your message. Your message is stored and waiting for your instructor when he or she reads their **e-mail**. In some courses, you can submit a book review, paper, quiz, or examination to a professor by **e-mail** and get it back, electronically marked and annotated. Computer screens are not the best way to read drafts, corrected papers or finished texts—always proofread papers from a printed copy. But you can easily convert **e-mail** messages into hard copy by clicking the print command on your software.

DOMAIN NAMES

.edu	school, college or university
.com	business or commercial enterprise
.gov	government office
.org	non-profit organization
.mil	military
.net	network or Internet service provider
.int	international organization

E-mail can add other dimensions to classroom discussion. For some shy students who feel uncomfortable speaking in front of classmates, e-mail provides a freer form of expression. More and more faculty use **e-mail** for journal writing, group projects, long distance communication between classes on different campuses, and other electronic activities that broaden the base of learning beyond the classroom. Some use specific kinds of software such as **WebCT** (http://www.webct.com/) or **BlackBoard** (http://www.blackboard.com/) to encourage collaborative writing in class where each student responds to a question raised by the teacher, then a broader online dialog that brings everyone into the discussion. **E-mail** addresses contain a logical structure that helps you to learn something about the sender. Each address takes the generic form of NAME@HOST.DOMAIN. The name before the @ symbol could be your actual name, a nickname, a set of numbers or initials or any tag that you use to identify yourself. Your campus mail **server** or commercial online service is the HOST. In the early years of **e-mail** usage, the standard three-letter designations for **DOMAIN** names after the period included extensions for private, public, and nonprofit organizations listed in the table.

DOMAIN NAMES ADDED IN 2001

.biz	business
.info	general information from an individual or company
.name	individual for personal use
.pro	professional--lawyer, physician, or accountant
.aero	airline, airport, air transport company, civil aviation
.coop	credit union or rural electric cooperative
.museum	museum with cultural or scientific focus

In 2001, due to increasing **e-mail** "traffic jams," new **domain** names were added to allow for continued expansion of **e-mail** and **Internet** addresses, especially for commercial businesses, individuals, professionals, and specialized organizations.

An **e-mail** address for someone who calls herself student at "state university" (student@stateuniv.edu) would read differently than if that same person had an account on America Online, a commercial service (student@aol.com).

Electronic Discussions

In its most widely used form, **e-mail** takes the form of traditional mail ("**snail mail**") in **digital** format. With the help of automated software programs (often generically called "**listservs**") such as **listserv**, **listproc**, mailbase, mailserv, and **majordomo**, **e-mail** can help to create communities of people with common interests. Such **e-mail** lists can be either unmoderated or moderated. An unmoderated list built around automated software sends out copies of every piece of **e-mail** sent to the list to each subscriber to that particular list. Obviously, this kind of system can lead to enormous amounts of **e-mail** that may prove entertaining but not very helpful. It can also allow some thoughtless individuals to engage in inappropriate language and comments that might lead to what **e-mail** aficionados refer to as a "flame war." Since most **e-mail** appears in text form, it becomes easy for both sender and receiver to misinterpret comments without the signal of facial gestures that allow us to interpret subtle shades of meaning in one-on-one personal conversations. **E-mail** courtesy ("netiquette") calls for careful use of words sometimes supplemented by the use of **"emoticons"** such as ; -) (a wink, a nose, and a smile to indicate humorous or joking intent) to help the recipient to make sense of some **e-mails**. For a good sampling of commonly used **emoticons**, see http://www.computeruser.com/resources/ dictionary/emoticons.html. Other forms of **e-mail** can be even more free flowing and open forums, such as **usenet newsgroups** or bulletin boards, **MOO's, MUD's** and chat rooms. Moderated **e-mail** lists tend to be more focused on a particular subject or interest, have some rules for subscriber writing, and employ the services of volunteer editors who direct discussions along thematic lines, rewrite **e-mails** for clarity and tact, and mediate among members of the list. This kind of list can create new communities of people interested in the same subjects or interests and prove ideal for discussions that are centered on a particular historical subject. These emerging social networks help students to learn how to discuss historical documents, research, and interpretations with one another, with their class instructors, and with instructors at other schools.

Listserv, listproc, or majordomo are software programs, or applications, making possible a discussion group on a local network or across the **Internet**. Participants subscribe, sending **e-mail** to a central account. From there, a list editor or the automated program function transmits the messages to everybody on the subscription list, hence the name **listserv**. You receive every message sent to the **listserv** as **e-mail**, either as a separate **e-mail** or in the form of a digest summarizing all the messages in a given day. **Listservs** can be modest – a professor setting one up just for your class – or extensive with subscribers from all over the world. A course-based **listserv** smoothes the way for electronic discussion before or after classroom discussion, since teacher and students can access all the postings and contribute comments as appropriate. **Listserv** postings might include pieces of historical evidence, assignments, inquiry questions, student papers, and discussion, with both teacher and students taking responsibility for placing primary documents and commentary on the list. Rather than the teacher assuming complete direction and control of the class discussion, use of a **listserv** can promote collaboration among students and between students and teacher.

Active learning replaces the passive learning of the traditional lecture class format.

Generally open to any subscriber, **listservs** address a variety of topics. A few convenient directories for locating specific lists among the thousands available for public subscription you might find useful include those in the following table.

LISTSERV INFORMATION AND DIRECTORIES

Discussion Groups: Mailing Lists (Library of Congress)
http://www.loc.gov/loc/guides/maillist.html

Internet & Networking: Internet Mailing Lists Guides and Resources (International Federation of Library Associations and Institutions)
http://www.ifla.org/I/training/listserv/lists.htm

CataList: The Official Catalog of LISTSERV Lists (L-Soft)
http://www.lsoft.com/catalist.html

Google Groups (Google.com)
http://groups.google.com/

Liszts: Directory of E-Mail Discussion Groups
http://www.liszts.com/

PAML: Publicly Accessible Mailing Lists (Neosoft)
http://paml.net/

Tile.Net/Newsgroup
http://www.tile.net/news/

Discussion Groups: Usenet Newsgroups
(Library of Congress)
http://www.loc.gov/loc/guides/news.html

More than 10,000 group conversations take place daily around the world on a part of the **Internet** called **Usenet Newsgroups**. **Usenet** is short for User Net. **Newsgroups** take the form of electronic bulletin boards, with messages listed in the order received. Generally, you read threads of discussion related to a particular topic, then comment upon the topic and previous postings by adding your own thoughts. For example, a newsgroup about the Vietnam War might have a series of postings about the

My Lai massacre. From there a new discussion string might begin about Hollywood movie portrayals of right and wrong in Vietnam. A related debate might develop about the treatment of Vietnam veterans back in the U.S. or about how the war looked through the eyes of Vietnamese peasants. This particular list has developed an extensive archive of postings available on the Web at http://www.lbjlib.utexas.edu/shwv/shwv-top.html.

Some **newsgroups** are moderated, but many are not. The quality of information posted can be very uneven, ranging from credible to incredible. But if you are skilled and careful in evaluating **newsgroups** and the materials posted, you can pick out important information and engage in surprisingly informed discussion with other group members.

You can set up, or configure, connections to **newsgroups** through graphical **browsers** like **Microsoft Internet Explorer**, **Netscape Navigator**, and the **Opera** browser. An established naming system for newsgroup addresses helps potential users identify the focus of discussion (e.g. news.soc.history.war.vietnam). In this example "news" is the protocol for newsgroup; "soc" is the top category dealing with society; "history" indicates the list has an historical rather than contemporary focus; and "war" and "vietnam" are hierarchies of sub-categories. Common abbreviations for top categories include:

NEWSGROUP CATEGORIES

alt	**Unusual topics, sometimes interesting and sometimes on the edge**
biz	**Business related topics**
comp	**Computer related topics**
humanities	**Arts, literature, philosophy**
misc	**Miscellaneous topics**
news	**Information about Usenet newsgroups**
rec	**Recreational interests and hobbies**
sci	**Scientific topics**
soc	**Social issues, including history**
talk	**Current issues**

Several search engines (e.g. Google) help make the passage relatively quick and painless to lists of **newsgroups** organized around topics of particular interest to you. If you are not ready to subscribe to a **newsgroup**, but need to find information on a particular topic, say for a class discussion, Google Groups (http://groups.google.com/) include current **Usenet** news information and an archive of its predecessor, DejaNews. This site can help you navigate through the maze of newsgroup postings to find very specific information that you need on any question. For example, in a Google Groups search field, I typed "Thaddeus Stevens," a Civil War and Reconstruction era member of Congress. Within seconds, I received a number of hot links to thoughtful postings that mused about "what if" questions. "What if" Stevens' plan after the Civil War to confiscate land from ex-planters and give it to ex-slaves had actually been approved by Congress? It was not approved, but if it had been, would the history of relations between races and sections in the United States have been different? Several thoughtful reflections on this "what if" question were the end result of my search.

Thousands of **listservs** and **newsgroups** serve as electronic discussion groups that bring together participants from many different locations. **BlackBoard**, **WebCT** or other classroom software facilitates discussion in a course; commercial online services (AOL, AT&T WorldNet, Compuserv, Earthlink, Mindspring, and Prodigy) offer forums similar in structure to **Usenet newsgroups**; **MOOs**, **MUDs**, and chat rooms create "virtual" environments for exploration; and Web-based forums make it possible to exchange graphics, hot links and multi-media WWW pages in addition to text messages.

H-NET: Humanities and Social Sciences Online

From **listservs** to **MOOs**, **Internet** sites offer a dazzling array of software-driven discussions. To the **Internet** beginner, this diversity of choices may seem overwhelming. For serious students of history, the central forum to investigate consists of the hundreds of scholarly networks brought together under the rubric of **H-Net: Humanities & Social Sciences OnLine** (http://www2.h-net.msu.edu/). For electronic discussions that are focused, easily available, reliable, and moderated by knowledgeable scholars, H-Net is the best place to start.

H-NET began as a series of humanities networks centered around specialized lists in various historical fields. Coordinated at the Matrix Center located at Michigan State University, H-NET sponsors and moderates over 130 electronic discussion lists and maintains affiliation with 11 more. Its forums range across geographical area studies (e.g. African, Asian, Australian, European, Latin American, Middle Eastern, and New Zealand history) to cultural studies (e.g. American popular culture and studies, Appalachia, Islamic Art and Architecture, Judaic studies, historic preservation, psychohistory, religious studies). Many networks focus on thematic approaches to history (e.g. business, childhood, diplomacy, the economy, education, the environment, film, intellectuals, labor, the law, immigration, the military, politics, public policy, religion, rural life, state building, urban studies, women and war, and women's history and studies). Lists include national histories of Britain and Ireland, the Caribbean, France, Germany, Italy, Japan, Mexico, Russia, Scandinavia, and Turkey. In addition to communities for those interested in educational technology, computers, **multimedia** and **CD-ROMs** a variety of lists address the history of California, Indiana, Maryland, Michigan, New Mexico, Ohio, Tennessee, and Texas. Networks devoted to United States history cover time periods (e.g. Colonial, Early Republic, Civil War, Gilded Age and Progressive, 1918-45), regional history (South and West), and new methods in social history about Native, African, immigrant, women, and working-class Americans. High school, college, and graduate students can join networks of fellow history students, while teachers can discuss teaching survey classes in political science and United States, Western Civilization, and World history (http://www2.h-net.msu.edu/teaching/). H-Net has much to offer history students from high school through college teaching, allowing students, researchers, and teachers the means to communicate with one another and build virtual communities across time, distance, and intellectual interests. In 1997, the American Historical Association awarded the James Harvey Robinson Prize for a history teaching aid to H-Net for the dedicated work of its hundreds of volunteer editors, a small paid staff, and members of its annually elected executive council.

H-Net lists all of these electronic forums at http://www2.h-net.msu.edu/lists/, while making subscribing to given lists as easy as clicking on a button and adding your name, institution, and **e-**

mail address. H-Net's **e-mail** lists function as electronic networks, linking professors, teachers and students in an egalitarian exchange of ideas and materials. Every aspect of academic life—research, teaching, controversies new and old—is open for discussion; decorum and mutual respect among lists members are maintained by H-Net's courteous and committed editors. You can receive individual messages as they are posted or in the form of a daily digest that includes all mailings for that day. Network logs are archived and searchable through a state-of-the-art **search engine** specially designed to build this ever-growing virtual library, archive, and message center into a true community of like-minded people.

Many items on each H-NET list are hot linked. Click H-LatAm and you will find yourself on the **home page** for an "international forum for the scholarly discussion of Latin American history." The page promises to enrich your study of Latin America by letting you subscribe to the forum, search its logs, read reviews of recent books, go to more online resources, and get timely information about conferences, journals, fellowships and relevant scholarship.

All H-NET networks are moderated by scholars to insure that discussion is respectful and that the material posted meets accepted academic criteria. You should not be overawed by this if you remember that a key part of H-NET's mission is "linking professors, teachers and students in an egalitarian exchange of ideas and materials."

Some H-Net lists have been active longer than others, giving them time and experience working with the electronic media of **e-mail**, Web sites, and **multimedia**. A few tie together the list and a corresponding professional association, such as H-SHGAPE (http://www2.h-net.msu.edu/~shgape/), the list dedicated to the discussion of the history of the Gilded Age and Progressive Era in U.S. History.

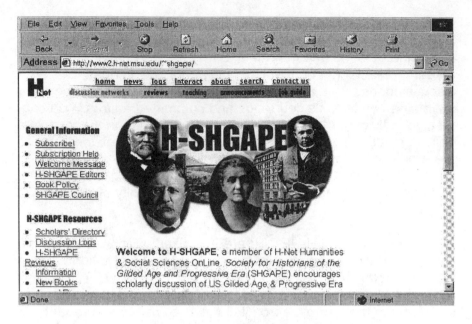

H-SHGAPE works closely with the Society for Historians of the Gilded Age and Progressive Era, a professional group of scholars, through the list and its Web site to coordinate recent developments in the subject area, alert members of both the list and the association about forthcoming events at historical conventions, provide online links to convention programs of the American Historical Association and the Organization of American Historians, post relevant information about the society and its elected officials, archive significant threads of discussion from the list, post sample class syllabi, maintain a library of book reviews, and keep an up-to-date page of **Internet** sites members will find helpful in their research, study, and teaching. Each H-Net list brings together a diverse set of members who customize their discussions, selected themes, organization, selection of books to review, and depth of its Web site depending on participants' interest, time, energy, and willingness to engage in community or network building.

H-Net has grown over the last few years to encompass a widening choice of materials and projects. The H-Net Reviews project (http://www2.h-net.msu.edu/reviews/) began by commissioning professional book reviews, then built an online archive of reviews.

It has since expanded into reviewing of articles, videos, **multimedia CD-ROMs**, Web sites, and computer software applications. The site can be searched by author, title, year of publication, publisher, reviewer, list, date of review, and keywords through a custom search function. Students should remember not to cut and paste or copy reviews, as this would constitute plagiarism, a serious form of academic misconduct that can lead to disciplinary punishments. The newly opened Academic Announcements site (http://www2.h-net.msu.edu/announce/) alerts history researchers and teachers about upcoming conferences, opportunities to present papers at professional meetings, new publications, workshops, funding for projects, and new Web sites. Graduate students and newly minted teachers will want to investigate the Job Guide (http://www2.h-net.msu.edu/jobs/) which lists employment opportunities in history and the humanities, the social sciences, and rhetoric and communications that used to appear only in professional association newsletters and the weekly *Chronicle of Higher Education*. The guide is searchable by discipline, subfield, state, country, institution, and keyword making sophisticated job searching as close as your computer keyboard. H-Net Reviews, Academic Announcements, and the Job Guide have quickly become vital, widely consulted professional tools used by students and teachers both around the nation and across the globe. H-Net has begun investigating creation of an online archive of historical images and sounds as well as custom publishing to keep availability and costs to students and teachers wide and inexpensive as the **digital** world permeates modern culture.

While no organization, real or virtual, can be a perfect democratic and electronic environment for breaking down barriers and enhancing communication between students and scholars, H-Net not only shows the promise and possibilities in new ways of studying and teaching history but also serves as a pioneering community of people interested in making new technologies inclusive, low in cost, and high in quality.

6. SEARCH ENGINES AND EVALUATING WEB SITES

Search Engines

Have you ever tried to find one small item in a large room—the proverbial needle in a haystack? It's not an easy task, unless you have sophisticated tools, in which case the odds improve greatly.

Let's play with the analogy. The sheer volume of text, images and sounds on the **World Wide Web** is like the large room or haystack. Search engines are the tools we can use to improve our chances of finding what we are looking for. A **search engine** is a powerful software program that searches out computer **servers** on the **Internet**, bringing back information that it then stores and sorts in a very complex database that you search to locate particular kinds of information. Yet with the tremendous growth of the **Internet** and millions of Web sites, we need to remember that only a small proportion of the total amount of information on the Web has been cataloged by search engines. In this still early stage of development, the **Internet** has no better mechanism that can serve as partial directories making it possible to find the needle in a vast haystack.

For all the power under the hood of an **Internet search engine**, it's only as good as (1) our ability to use it, and (2) the classification system it uses to organize all the information it gathers. Each **search engine** has a different way of arranging knowledge, so no one engine is the best one to use for all purposes. Each has strengths and weaknesses depending on what we are trying to locate and how we try to find it.

Internet search engines and directories get their data in one of two ways. (1) Creators of sites register their pages, supplying the **URL**, a summary of the site's contents, and key words that users might associate with the substantive data. (2) Automated computer programs, variously called "bots," "robots," "spiders," or "Web crawlers," continually search the Web for new and updated pages, following links from site to site. In this way, the spider spins its computer Web, crawling through millions of pages to collect data which it updates on a regular basis. Yet as sites go out of

48

operation and addresses change, Web crawlers cannot possibly keep up with the rapidly growing amount of new sites, reorganized sites, renamed and readdressed locations, and Web sites that become "dead links" once operators no longer maintain them or they are taken offline.

Once a WWW **search engine** collects all this data, it must process findings in ways that make the information accessible to Web users. Hundreds of different **search engines** exist to assist you in locating materials. A good place to start would be the Library of Congress guide to Locating Information on the Internet (http://www.loc.gov/loc/guides/locate.html) that lists major subject directories and **search engines** you can use. Perhaps the most widely known **search engine**, Yahoo! (http://www.yahoo.com/) organizes information into general categories. In contrast, Alta Vista (http://www.altavista.com/) functions as a raw but voluminous index. However, its search capacities can be refined. A third search site, Excite (http://www.excite.com/), sorts information by concepts. The hottest **search engine** among many computer scientists as of 2001 is Google (http://www.google.com/) which claims to index more Web sites and pages than any other **search engine** or directory. The Northern Light (http://www.northernlight.com/) **search engine** proves very effective in conducting focused searches on scholarly topics, organizing the results in a very useful manner. For information on the other hundreds of **search engines** and directories, take a look at the Search Engine Watch (http://www.searchenginewatch.com).

The best way to understand differences among search engines is to experiment with doing a particular search to determine which engine best suits your purposes for that task. You can connect to these five **search engines** and many others by clicking the search button on your **browser**. As software companies update browsers such as **Microsoft Internet Explorer**, **Netscape Navigator,** and **Opera**, the specific **search engines** which each uses changes as existing ones are improved, absorbed, or replaced by newer **search engine**s.

Type the word "holocaust" in the white search boxes of each of these **search engines** and you will get a good sense of the differences and similarities. Press the return key and you will get a list of hot links. On Yahoo!, you get twenty-six category matches.

The category scheme goes from main topic to sub categories. Here are examples, all of which are hot-linked.

AN EXAMPLE OF HOW <u>YAHOO!</u> LISTS CATEGORIES

Arts > Humanities > History > By Time Period > 20th Century > Holocaust, The

Entertainment > Movies and Film > Titles > Drama > Historical > Holocaust

Arts > Humanities > History > By Time Period > 20th Century > Holocaust, The > Memorials > United States Holocaust Memorial Museum

Society and Culture > Religion and Spirituality > Faiths and Practices > Judaism > Holidays and Observances > Yom Hashoah – Holocaust Remembrance Day

Entertainment > Movies and Film > Titles > Horror > Psychos > Cannibals > Cannibal Holocaust

Entertainment > Movies and Film > Titles > Documentary > Arts and Humanities > History > 20th Century > Holocaust

Business and Economy > Shopping and Services > Books > Booksellers > History > Titles > Holocaust, The

---

By contrast, a search on Alta Vista provided 517,255 results — impressive numbers, but unmanageable. By refining the search, let's say to "holocaust and gypsies," the volume reduced to five results, including two scholarly bibliographies listing books about the impact of the Holocaust on the Roma ("gypsie" is a derogatory slang term) people of Central Europe.

The same search on Excite yielded 273,924 links to Web sites like the United States Holocaust Museum in Washington, D.C.; Yad Vashem: The Holocaust Martyrs' and Heroes' Remembrance Authority in Jerusalem; and the Simon Wiesenthal Center in Los Angeles, California. At the bottom of the search results page, you will find "Sponsored Links," a reflection of the fact that most commercial **search engines** now collect payment from clients who wish their sites to receive favorable, more high profile listing on the site. The number of primary results from these three commercial **search engines** can easily overwhelm a researcher, while the secondary results are both mixed and at times rather disappointing.

A search of "Holocaust" at the Google **search engine** brings up 1,030,000 results, but notice that the early results tend to be from credible, scholarly sites that a serious student and researcher would want to encounter first rather than Hollywood movie sites, videos, and films about cannibals. A good researcher would further refine the search and visit some of the Web pages listed, looking for links to still more relevant sites. Let's say that your search has carried you down a path of links that have helped you define a topic for a hypothetical research paper, for example, the controversy swirling around Daniel J. Goldhagen's book, *Hitler's Willing Executioners* (1996). Now, you can do a much more focused probe. If you type in the name of the author and/or his book in the search box of any engine, the links generated will be both rich and manageable. Such a search on the Google site, brings up a rich, detailed, and scholarly discussion from H-German, one of the H-Net discussion lists involving expert scholars rather than "Holocaust revisionists" who make stupendous claims that the Holocaust never happened on the basis of flawed logic, thin evidence, and some readers' gullibility.

Now try the same search about "Holocaust" at the Northern Light site. You obtain 489,415 results organized immediately into "Custom Search Folders" arranged by subject or category in the form of blue results folders. Depending on the nature and scope of your search, certain folders will prove more helpful than others among the listed categories including "Special Collection documents," "Jewish Holocaust (Shoah)," "Concentration camps," "Public monuments," "Teachers & Teaching," "Torah & Talmud," "Wiesel, Elie," "Insurance industry," "Pope John Paul II," "U.S. House of Representatives," "Methadone," "Internet," and "all others." Clicking on any one of the subject folders takes you to another more detailed set of folders broken down further by subject area, allowing for access to in-depth primary sources, published memoirs, scholarly accounts, and a host of research materials that would add to the research material previously gathered by a trip to your school's library.

While Yahoo!, Alta Vista, and Excite are well known and commonly used **search engines**, in this particular example, the Google and Northern Light searches provided a more useful, focused set of search results that would not require the hours or days of sifting through the huge amounts of data provided by the more general engines that are extremely helpful for shoppers, general readers, and **Internet** surfers looking for brief summaries of what history students and teachers soon learn is a challenging, complicated subject with many angles of research to explore.

Search engines can be powerful teaching tools. A number of college instructors have developed courses where students build **hypertext** links and paths of understanding about holocausts/genocides/massacres. For example, students at Father Ryan, a Roman Catholic high school in Nashville, Tennessee have created a Web site (http://www.fatherryan.org/frhsonline/foreman/) for their class on the Holocaust that includes not only the class syllabus, teacher expectations, and prayers for victims of the Holocaust, but also a section on links to some of the best Web sites on the Holocaust including the Holocaust History Project, the Nizkor Project, the Visual History Foundation's Survivors of the Shoah, and the Fortunoff Video Archive of Holocaust Testimonies at Yale University.

A search on the "Nanking Massacre" at the Google and Northern Light sites produced rich results with links to a disturbing, gruesome collection of pictures from the public **domain** at Princeton University, book reviews available for reading or purchase online, and immersion in the ongoing controversies regarding atrocities by the Japanese Imperial Army in China and Korea during World War II and links to discussion of genocide, warfare, the rewriting of Japanese history books about the period, and more topics worth careful study and research.

In the 1937 Nanking Massacre, the Japanese occupiers reportedly raped 20,000 women and murdered 300,000 residents. This is a frightening but important topic. Searches joining the words "rape and holocaust," "rape and Bosnia," "ethnic cleansing," and "rape and slavery" can help us gain some insight into the history, politics, and mass pathology of such hideous human behavior. Sorry for all the gory detail, but the examples showcase how

52

search engines can be used as a learning tool. In addition to Yahoo!, Alta Vista, Excite, Google, and Northern Light, hundreds of other **search engine** can be found. HotBot is notable for the amount of data it stores and its easy-to-use options to distill searches. Most sophisticated, well-funded sites, like the Library of Congress, come complete with engines to search their collections.

Many colleges and universities have **search engines** on their **home page** to help you locate specific colleges, departments, programs, libraries, faculty and students. Yet as the **Internet** evolves, troubling questions about privacy and confidentiality must be thought about carefully in order to serve those using Web sites and protect people who have not given permission to list personal information such as names, **e-mail** addresses, telephone numbers, home and school addresses, departmental majors, and sometimes very specific student identification numbers.

Many Web search tools give you a variety of options and resources: specialized searches of images, audio and video by year and geographical areas; directories of libraries, phone numbers, street addresses, detailed maps, and **e-mail** listings; and even customized channels to receive news, stock quotes, sports news, TV listings or information on subjects of your choosing. The ability to refine this information and deepen searches differs from **search engine** to **search engine**. Each **search engine** usually has a Help button that you can click for instructions. Be sure to read the Help section before doing any searches at that site.

Web crawlers and **search engines** have an enormous capacity to put resources on your desktop. But just like a car with immense horsepower, these engines don't drive themselves. Searching is a human skill: an extension of our intellectual ability to gather and organize knowledge. Understood in this way, **Internet** search tools become powerful, socially-driven engines of human inquiry.

Evaluating Web Sites

In the wake of the computer and knowledge revolution of the last two decades, we need to remember that information is not the same as knowledge. Information is raw data that has not been filtered through the intellectual process of thought, evaluation, and interpretation. Knowledge comes from intellectual judgment based on examination of factual evidence, experience with a range of primary and secondary sources, and the context of what kind of evidence exists, who created it, and why. Just because we find information on the Web doesn't mean it's true. Lots of inaccurate factual evidence, ill-formed interpretations, and **multimedia** evidence without context can be found on the **Internet**. How do we evaluate the results of our searches and decide what we find is worth serious consideration and use?

This problem of how to transform information into knowledge is not unique to the Web. Verification of evidence is essential to the study of history. A historian finding a narrative about slavery would ask questions about its source, authenticity, point of view, context, relevance and much more. Those kinds of questions apply whether we find the information on the **World Wide Web**, in a book, or in someone's attic.

Information found on the Web can just as easily come from someone's vanity page, a scanned document, reference works, or a rich scholarly archive. We can and should evaluate Web sites to determine their credibility and usefulness as tools for historical learning. Is the **domain** a college or university (edu)? An international institution (int)? A government agency (gov)? A nonprofit organization (org)? A military site (mil)? A business (com or biz)? A firm or individual (inf)? Do we know who the author is and what they know about the topic of the site? Is the author the same as the webmaster, or are they two different people? Does he or she provide us with an **e-mail** address hot link and hopefully more information about personal qualifications and professional education and credentials, so that we can make judgments about the credibility of the site? Experienced Web editors often provide a brief biography or a full resume about their qualifications for operating the Web site. At the top or bottom of the **home page** of the site, does the editor tell us when the site was last updated or revised? Are hot links on each page labeled accurately, giving credit to whomever created that site or has the editor renamed external sites with names that do not match the **home page** when you click on the hot link(s)?

While historians have been slow to develop criteria and tools to evaluate Web sites, professional librarians have been hard at work developing online primers for evaluating information on the **Internet**. Librarians trained in how to find, use, and evaluate different kinds of information agree that at least five criteria should be examined to evaluate any source of information: Authority, Accuracy, Objectivity, Currency, and Coverage.

Authority. Who is the author, an expert or a novice? How do you know? Can you contact the author at an **e-mail** address, college, company or organizational address? Is the information published under the auspices of a scholarly or academic institution? A commercial enterprise? A personal homepage? Can you ascertain the relationship between the author and the publishing body (e.g. A faculty member or a student at a university, an experienced professional, a respected figure in their field)?

Accuracy. Does the author or editor present factually based information, citing the sources of that information? Does the language seem to depend on personal opinion that is not supported by reliable, accurate documentation? If primary sources, images, and sounds are used, are they placed within any broader historical context to help you understand their origin, purpose, and meaning?

Objectivity. Does the Web site and/or author providing the information have a commercial, political, economic, social, or philosophical agenda? Is only one kind of information about the subject presented or are there alternate perspectives supported by reliable factual information, logical argument, and reasoned presentation or does the author try to advocate a cause or persuade you of one point of view?

Currency. How up to date is the site? Does the homepage indicate the last date of updating or revision? Does the author locate his or her work in a larger body of literature and scholarship? Can you tell where documents, sources, and interpretations come from, when they were developed, and why? When dates appear, are they current or appropriate to the historical period? All too many Web sites are created, then abandoned without any attempt to update the materials. Conscientious editors will tell you when and how often the site is updated or if it has not been maintained since a particular date.

Coverage. How extensive is the site? Do the latest technical innovations substitute for or complement substantive content? Has the editor kept the length of each Web page reasonable and focused on the topic for that page? Do hot links on the site refer you to a range of sources including printed texts, images, sounds, **multimedia**, reference works, lists of additional reliable works (bibliographies), and other Web sites? If a site refers mostly to internal links to other parts of that site, is this due to a tight focus on the subject at hand or an unwillingness to encourage you to consider other sources, arguments, and points of view?

New, expert, and scholarly are not necessarily better than old, novice and commercial or personal. A point of view does not necessarily invalidate information. Nevertheless, all of these questions help you to put in context and evaluate the information you find. Sites mentioned in the box below are good places to learn about evaluating what you discover online. We could ask many more questions; however, you are encouraged to involve yourself in the process of interrogating Web sources and evidence.

LIBRARIANS CAN HELP YOU TO EVALUATE ONLINE INFORMATION

Jan Alexander and Marsha Ann Tate, "Evaluating Web Resources"
(Widener University Library)
http://www2.widener.edu/Wolfgram-Memorial-Library/webevaluation/webeval.htm

Esther Grassian, "Thinking Critically about World Wide Web Resources"
(University of California, Los Angeles College Library)
http://www.library.ucla.edu/libraries/college/help/critical/index.htm

Robert Harris, "Evaluating Internet Research Sources,"
http://www.virtualsalt.com/evalu8it.htm

Jim Kapoun, "Teaching undergrads WEB Evaluation: A guide for library instruction"
(Association of College and Research Libraries)
http://www.ala.org/acrl/undwebev.html

LIBRARIANS CAN HELP YOU TO EVALUATE ONLINE INFORMATION, continued

Elisabeth E. Kirk, "Evaluating Information Found on the Internet" (Milton S. Eisenhower Library, Johns Hopkins University)
http://milton.mse.jhu.edu:8001/research/education/net.html

7. STUDENT PAPERS—PUTTING HISTORY ON LINE

Student Uses of the Net

Historians work with primary sources such as letters, diaries, journals, personal and institutional records, government documents, published articles and books, and other text-based materials. Yet we know that sights and sounds can also serve as materials to aid us in making sense of the past. While still only in a very early stage from the view of an historical researcher, the **Internet** can provide access to a diversity of source materials that students and teachers can make use of in and outside the classroom to make history alive and exciting. Much of primary source material available on the **Internet** comes in the form of raw data with little or no context provided, so it must be used with care. Web sites serve as archives to store primary sources; as library catalogs giving access to basic information about sources, journals, and books; and as **multimedia** stations giving selective opening to sights and sounds in the form of paintings, still pictures, film clips, motion pictures, and collections of sound files **digitally** converted from older, obsolete technologies.

This Day in History

An interesting and fun way to enter the historical arena involves relating today's date with events in world history. Among the best of these "Today in History" sites are the American Memory site at the Library of Congress (http://lcweb2.loc.gov/ammem/today/today.html) which includes primary source texts, pictures, and hotlinks to related materials in the extensive Library of Congress holdings. The Associated Press in cooperation with the New York Times newspaper sponsors a daily site (http://www.nytimes.com/aponline/national/AP-History.html) relating events over the broad sweep of history that occurred on a particular day, while the same newspaper publishes an online site listing events on that day along with an image of a front page from the paper for an event that happened "On This Day" (http://www.nytimes.com/learning/general/onthisday/index.html). For well-written, reliable biographical information about people in U.S. history, you can consult the online supplements to the ***American National***

Biography series published by Oxford University Press (http://www.anb.org/) that include further readings useful for research papers, while short biographies of people in world history can be found at the Biography.com commercial site (http://www.biography.com/) hosted by the Arts & Entertainment television network.

Primary Text Sources

Students and teachers find that history comes alive when they have the opportunity to see, read, think about, and debate the actual texts that politicians, diplomats, and military leaders at various points in time wrote. While **Internet** sites are only beginning to provide these kinds of sources, excellent places to mine such materials include the Library of Congress' lesson on "The Historian's Sources" (http://lcweb2.loc.gov/learn/lessons/psources/pshome.html) and the University of Idaho's listing of "Repositories of Primary Sources" (http://www.uidaho.edu/special-collections/Other.Repositories.html). *Reading About the World: A Reader for the Study of World Civilizations* (http://www.wsu.edu:8080/~wldciv/world_civ_reader/), the World History Archives (http://www.hartford-hwp.com/archives/index.html), and World History (http://www2.tntech.edu/history/world.html) provide access to sources for world history courses. Students in Western civilization courses will find extensive primary sources at the EuroDocs site sponsored by Brigham Young University (http://www.lib.byu.edu/~rdh/eurodocs/index.html). Sources in United States history can be found all over the **Internet**. Among some of the higher quality sites, be sure to examine the Avalon Project at Yale Law School (http://www.yale.edu/lawweb/avalon/avalon.htm) encompassing documents in history, law, and foreign policy, the Making of America project at the University of Michigan (http://moa.umdl.umich.edu/) focusing on 8,500 books and 50,000 journal articles in nineteenth-century American social history, and the Chronology of U.S. Historical Documents at the University of Oklahoma College of Law (http://www.law.ou.edu/hist/).

More and more private archives and government agencies are providing historical sources on Web sites from the papers of U.S. presidents through manuscript collections of historical actors such as Susan B. Anthony, Emma Goldman, Samuel Gompers, Robert

E. Lee, and U.S. Grant. Some ambitious Web editors have placed entire collections of scanned papers and books online. A few of the best such projects are the Electronic Text Center at the University of Virginia (http://etext.lib.virginia.edu/uvaonline.html), Project Gutenberg (http://www.gutenberg.net/), and the Online Books Page (http://digital.library.upenn.edu/books/). Many archives are rushing to place manuscript inventories, samples of primary documents, and contact information on Web sites, but no central site exists to coordinate these archival efforts. One place to begin is the Library Catalogs and Archives page (http://www2.tntech.edu/history/libs.html). Several good places to find online library catalogs include LibDex: The Library Index (http://www.libdex.com/), Gabriel: Gateway to Europe's National Libraries (http://portico.bl.uk/gabriel/en/countries.html), and Online Library Card Catalogs in Asia (http://www.pitt.edu/%7Eealib/libcat.htm) from the East Asian Library at the University of Pittsburgh. When conducting a search for book sources for a research paper, you can access the online catalogs of major public libraries in Boston, Chicago, Cleveland, and New York as well as thousands of specialized academic libraries that your teacher can suggest.

The Sounds of the Past

Perhaps the most exciting possibilities for studying history via the **Internet** come with the increasing number of sites dedicated to providing **multimedia** sources including sound files, video clips, and in a few cases even feature-length motion pictures. At Michigan State University, scholars have begun the National Gallery of the Spoken Word project (http://www.ngsw.org/) to create an archive of twentieth-century sounds in U.S. history, while the Vincent Voice Library at Michigan State (http://www.lib.msu.edu/vincent/) contains recordings from the last one hundred years of American history. One of the earliest such projects that began at Northwestern University evolved into the History and Politics Out Loud site (http://www.hpol.org/) containing sounds from U.S. presidents Franklin D. Roosevelt, John F. Kennedy, Lyndon B. Johnson, Richard Nixon, and Bill Clinton; civil rights activists A. Philip Randolph, Whitney Young, Martin Luther King, Jr., John Lewis, Roy Wilkins; and world political leaders such as Winston Churchill and Nikita Khrushchev. Reaching further afield, the British Library has assembled the National Sound

Archive (http://www.bl.uk/collections/sound-archive/cat.html) of over 2.5 million sounds, while the Rock & Roll Hall of Fame and Museum in Cleveland, Ohio (http://www.rockhall.com/) samples the music that transformed post-World War II American culture.

Visual Sources

Still photographs, film clips, and feature films can be found in abundance on a host of Web sites. Corbis (http://www.corbis.com/), a Microsoft Corporation subsidiary, may have the best still photograph collection on the **Internet** which includes the well-known Bettman Archive of black and white stills. The Library of Congress has fully searchable sites (http://www.loc.gov/harvest/query-lc.html) for photographs and film clips that will repay patience in learning how to use the search function. One of the library's most interesting collections is the America from the Great Depression to World War II: Photographs from the FSA [Farm Security Administration] /OWI [Office of War Information], 1935-1945 site, part of the American Memory project which hopes to place a large sampling of the national library's historic record online for all citizens to use and enjoy. Specialized sites such at the Great War Photos site (http://www.ukans.edu/~kansite/ww_one/photos/greatwar.htm) include not only military technology, politicians, generals, and diplomats, but also rank and file soldiers, shots of the environmental impact of total war, and some shocking images of modern war. European museums cooperated to arrange a site (http://www.art-ww1.com/) dedicated to remembering the eightieth anniversary of the signing of the Armistice that ended that war. The online site of the Chicago Public Schools (http://www.cpsart.org/wpa.lasso) has posted a wonderful exhibit of Works Progress Administration murals in local schools. The Newsfilm Library site at the University of South Carolina (http://www.sc.edu/newsfilm/) contains over eleven million feet of Twentieth Century Fox Movietone newreels from the 1919-1934 and 1942-1944 periods. Modern-day Web sites for commercially released motion pictures that can be gleaned from your television set screen will one day serve as fodder for future cultural and film historians.

Possibilities for Multimedia History

The challenge facing both students and teachers in history classes remains how to make good use of this rapidly expanding universe of source materials. Primary documents, electronic texts, photographs, sounds, and film clips can be used to create lively classroom experiences, engage people in the process of historical research, teach them the fine points of historical methodology, and encourage the development of critical thinking through the integration of text, sound, and sight in ways that earlier generations of historians could only dream about. An increasing number of teachers are experimenting with new classroom teaching that sometimes includes the creation of Web sites either by individual students or by teams of students working to build a collaborative project from start to finish. Oftentimes, students know more about the technical details of creating such sites than their instructors who are more experienced at the art of historical interpretation that takes information from a variety of sources to create new knowledge. Together, students and teachers can make history an enlivening, relevant, fun, and satisfying learning experience.

Constructing Web Sites

Virtually anybody can create a Web page that displays your work to the world. Knowing that peers, family, friends, and countless others will see your work provides a good incentive to do your best work. Remember that talented, thoughtful individuals sometimes produce more interesting sites than multi-billion dollar corporations. Often, young students design better Web history than credentialed scholars. Of course anyone can build **digital** trash or a minor work of art. History-oriented Web sites come in all sizes, designs, structures, depth, and usability ranging from a one-page personal statement to a sophisticated, far-ranging examination of multiple historical topics. The more you surf the web, the more experienced you will become in judging the quality, strengths, and weaknesses of different Web sites. Some serve as virtual archives and libraries providing you with lots of textual, audio, and visual information in its rawest form—as primary documents, articles, and books. Other sites present highly interpretive points of view using primary and secondary documents and the **multimedia** capability of the Net to present powerful, sophisticated, and thought-provoking historical interpretations. A few scholars have created extensive sites collecting material from around the world to help others or focused sites around a particular historical period, topic, or problem to teach students the art of historical interpretation.

In the last decade, elegant, easy-to-use Web-authoring software has made it possible for non-technical users to design an **Internet** site. Software that you can download for free or a minimal price right off the Web is already changing how students do research projects from K-12 through college. Go to any of the major **search engine** sites, type in "**HTML** editor," and you will get a list of all kinds of Web site software. Somewhere on the list, you will see such major programs as Macromedia's Dreamweaver, Microsoft's FrontPage, Sausage Software's HotDog, and Soft Quad's HoTMetaL. Your school may have a preferred Web editing package, so be sure to check with your local computer laboratory help desk or the information technology staff.

There is nothing terribly mysterious about **HTML**, **Hyper Text Markup Language**, the standard programming language for Web pages. Let's assume that you connect to a hypothetical Web site that reads:

MY HISTORY PROJECT

This **home page** of my first **Internet** research project includes links to related Web sites.

If you are using the **Microsoft Internet Explorer** browser, you can now go to the View menu, scroll down and then click Source. A page then appears with our hypothetical site's **HTML** document structure.

<html>

<head>

<title>MY HISTORY PROJECT</title>

</head>

```
<body>
```

This **home page** of my first **Internet** research project includes links to related Web sites.

```
</body>
```

```
</html>
```

The View Source function reveals **HTML** tags (like <body>) that define the look and face of a document. The <html> and </html> tags, written in **HTML** code, frame the opening <html> and closing </html> of this simple **HTML** document. The <head> and <body> tags represent the header and the body of the document. Note that each set of **HTML** tags comes in pairs that are "turned on" <N> and "turned off" </N>. **HTML** coding is quite similar to clicking on and off for special functions such as Bold, Italicize, or Underline in a word processing program. You turn on a function with the open tag, and turn it off with the closing tag. Other tags encode bold face, italics, centering, headings and subheadings, hot links, images, animation, meta tags, addresses, dividing lines and other more detailed information about additional features onto a Web page. Anybody, with a glossary of tags in front of them and tutoring in the most basic of **HTML** writing skills, can produce a basic Web page easily and quickly. Yet inserting **HTML** tags can be an extraordinarily labor-intensive and very boring process. For basic text documents, most recent versions of the leading word processing programs include the option to save documents as Web pages or **HTML** documents. As **HTML** coding becomes increasingly more complex with frames and cascading style sheets, learning how to code **HTML** by hand has become more difficult and time consuming. Many **Internet** sites exist to provide **HTML** lessons and tag charts. A good place to start is the Bare Bones Guide to HTML (http://werbach.com/barebones/).

Fortunately, **HTML** editors—many available for free or as shareware on the Web—provide templates, or models, that allow you to start with a basic Web page that can be built quickly by typing in your title, heading(s), and text and placing images between the appropriate tags. Go to any of the major **search engine** sites, type in "**HTML** editors," and you will find many excellent, easy-to-use Web editing programs. Some are free, some require payment after a trial period ("shareware"), and some are very sophisticated commercial programs that cost a bit more.

For those who have little interest in becoming Web geeks, shortcuts can make your work easy. By clicking on the View menu and the Source option—as we did above—you can see the code of any Web document. If you like what you see, you can borrow and revise for your own page. Borrowing is part of the accepted culture of the Web, as long as it's done for simple **HTML** scripts on a modest scale. Modest means that you don't obtain someone's sophisticated sound, video or animation program without permission. Public domain clip art, images, animation and sound can be found at many sites that you can locate by typing in keywords at a **search engine** and following the links. If you have questions about "fair use" of intellectual property, go to the Copyright Website (http://www.benedict.com/). Whenever you place a link to someone else's work, be sure to acknowledge their effort and original work by citing the exact title, person, and institution in parentheses next to the link on your site. Cooperation between Web site editors has made possible the growth of an astounding array of historical material on the **Internet**, such as the sites mentioned in this work.

You do not have to know anything about **HTML** codes if you use software programs such as Dreamweaver, FrontPage, HoTMetaL, or HotDog which empower you to build your own Web site complete with links, images, animation, sound, and text documents almost as easily as you would a word processing document. Later versions of **Netscape Navigator** come with the Composer function on the Tasks menu that allow for basic **HTML** coding and Web site editing.

Creating Online History

As Web-authoring tools become easier to use, student **multimedia** projects multiply. While oftentimes students pick up the ability to use such programs quickly, they can become overly enamored with the program, forgetting that it is the means to creating good history. Teachers will want to think carefully about how best to create Web-based assignments, provide clear and precise guidelines, work with information technology people on campus, and show students how to synthesize primary sources such as texts, images, and sounds to take advantage of the possibilities that **multimedia** history can provide.

One of the best examples of how students and teachers can learn and practice the art of historical interpretation is the New Deal Network (http://newdeal.feri.org/) which began as a small site connected to the Franklin D. Roosevelt Presidential Library, then expanded as teachers and students participated in Web-based projects in local communities. Director Tom Thurston identified, selected, and prepared documents in **HTML** coding and photographs from the Roosevelt Library, the National Archives, and other repositories to create the New Deal Document Library. The Classroom section includes lesson plans, guides, and sample student projects such as the superbly executed FDR Cartoon Archive (http://www.nisk.k12.ny.us/fdr/) built by students at Niskayuna High School in New York state. The site includes a hotlink to the H-US1918-45 network of scholars who contribute to the H-Net community on interwar U.S. history as well as featured selections picked by director Tom Thurston who constantly looks for new additions for the site. To date, featured segments encompass letters to Mrs. Eleanor Roosevelt, the Tennessee Valley Authority, the Civilian Conservation Corps, selections from the Works Progress Administration slave narratives, scholarly essays on student activism and works in labor history, and articles from *The Survey* and *Survey Graphic* about social conditions and welfare policies of the time. The Links section includes samples of course syllabi, student projects, related Web sites, and connections to a host of valuable sources on Depression-era history.

Building such a thoughtful, in-depth history site did not happen quickly—it took years of effort by hundreds of people. Over time, people who lived through the Great Depression of the 1930s, students, teachers, scholars, archivists, librarians, and computer specialists learned to cooperate with one another. Primary sources such as documents, photographs, transcribed oral history interviews, paintings, posters, and other materials were identified, located, examined, and collected. Students learned how to engage in historical research with primary sources, while teachers discovered that students find hands-on projects with state-of-the-art computer technology such as scanners, software, personal computers, Web editing programs, and loading materials to the site's computer **server** exciting. Computer literacy, the examination and study of visual sources, the art of bringing together a variety of sources, and working together as part of a community all came together into an innovative, useful, and growing project that brings historical understanding of the Depression, New Deal reforms, and the social history of the 1930s to people across the country.

Student web-based projects can range from the simple and quick to the complex and lengthy. Transcription of oral history interviews or scanning of local newspapers, magazine articles, letters, diaries, and papers reveal the importance of primary sources. Seeking out and making sense of visual images leads to new ways of thinking while promoting the kind of visual literacy that is rapidly becoming a necessity in today's modern world. Integrating paintings, drawings, maps, posters, recorded speeches, and the sounds of a world now gone can teach students to realize that direct, personal experience may be only one form of learning while helping teachers to consider overlooked sources and new ways of thinking about historical periods and topics that once appeared to be long settled by published scholars. Shrewdly designed class assignments expose students to historical methodology, computer and visual literacy, and the relationship between sources, logic, and interpretation as a way of thinking. Rather than "covering material or periods," teachers become guides rather than all powerful authority figures. Collaborative learning empowers students, building confidence along with intellectual and practical skills.

To date, teachers have only begun experimenting with ways to use the **Internet** for classroom learning and historical research. When you begin your first **Internet**-based assignment, start simple, realizing that much of the material on Web sites consists of raw data—information—that must be studied, analyzed, and combined into knowledge and understanding of the past. Your teacher might start by asking you to find primary sources online, then move on to using these sources for an oral presentation, a research paper, or an extended project with fellow students. A class research paper can be enriched by links to documents, **digital** images, and footnotes. Be careful not to download someone else's work and claim it as your own—that would be plagiarism, a serious form of academic misconduct. For a good guide to citing **Internet** sources in footnotes and bibliography, check out Mel Page's "A Brief Citation Guide for Internet Sources in History and the Humanities" (http://www2.h-net.msu.edu/about/citation/). While some Web sites claim to offer "sample papers" for sale at a high price, most are poorly done, based on outdated materials, and written in a style quite unlike your own. While plagiarism—taking credit for work you did not do—is a potential risk, the possibilities of the **Internet** to enhance historical understanding vastly outweigh such risk.

Web-authoring tools are glitzy computer toys, while many Web sites provide the latest "bells and whistles" without much thoughtful substance. When online sources are used creatively and well, however, history students can turn them into serious scholarly instruments to reconstruct the past. If you have an interesting idea, consult with your teacher who may prove intrigued by something that had never occurred to her. Cooperating with other students and your teacher will boost your self-confidence, give you marketable skills in high demand, teach you the value of cooperative effort, and enhance the classroom experience for everyone.

8. MULTIMEDIA HISTORY: SIGHTS, SOUNDS, AND CD-ROMs

CD-ROMs and History

As visual media such as motion pictures, television, and **Internet** Web sites have entered mainstream American culture, students have grown accustomed to thinking of history as a **multimedia** experience involving sights and sounds as well as the traditional focus on written or printed texts. Teachers have not always kept up with the rapidly moving developments in instructional technology that now make it possible for students to study history on their own as individuals and members of small groups, as an extracurricular part of the classroom setting, and in cooperation with teachers as "guides on the side" over the usual "sage on the stage" role. Yet historians still rightly insist on the importance of identification, collection, reading, and analysis of sources as the best way to build historical interpretations worth taking seriously. At times a generational divide between computer-savvy students and teachers suffering from technophobia makes it difficult to take advantage of advances in new instructional technology. One way of moving beyond this divide would be to rediscover the value of texts using new technology, while introducing sights and sounds through a medium that one person can learn to use at an appropriate pace. The possibilities of **multimedia** history can best be seen through the use of **CD-ROMs—Compact Discs with Read-Only Memory**.

CD-ROM technology is now over a generation old, but stills presents the opportunity to distribute large amounts of information in a compact size at an affordable price. One CD can store 650 MB of data, the equivalent of 300,000 typed pages or 100 million words—a potentially vast storehouse in which students of history can pack huge text files that would fill many books; large-sized, high resolution photographs; sizable sound files, and extensive video or film clips. Most personal computers now come with **CD-ROM** drives built in, while many students employ CD-W drives to write, or "burn," customized CDs for musical listening and class projects. The large volume capacity of a single CD makes this medium an ideal candidate for **multimedia** history.

CD-ROMs for Text Storage and Retrieval

Since CDs have been used for music recording and computer games for the entire lifetime of today's students, the medium is a familiar one to students. Even longtime teachers feel comfortable with this mode of storage. Many students grow up having learned eye-hand coordination through the use of computer games and commercially produced educational software. Government agencies, private publishers, and some enterprising teachers now realize that **CD-ROMs** make for a perfect way to amass large amounts of information in a seamless database that anyone can manipulate to good effect. For example, the United States Government Printing Office has begun an extensive campaign to make public domain government documents available to the public at very low prices. In 1998, the United States Army's Center of Military History in Washington, D.C. decided to reprint as three **CD-ROMs** its history of *The United States Army in World War I, 1917-1919*, originally published between 1988 and 1992 in seventeen durable, but costly clothbound volumes. Adding to the attractively low $20 price, this publication also includes supplementary materials such as the five-volume *Order of Battle of the United States Land Forces in the World War* (originally published 1931-1949), the American Battle Monuments Commission's *American Armies and Battlefields in Europe* (first published in 1938), a sixteen-print set of *Army Art of World War I*, and a modern introduction by military historian Kenneth Hamburger to place the documents in context.

Modern textbooks used in U.S. history survey classes often gloss over military history, so students can use this collection that would cost hundreds of dollars from a book store specializing in rare and out of print books to read primary sources from American Expeditionary Force commanders down to after-action reports by field commanders who fought with the French and British armies and participated in the independent U.S. operations at the battles of St. Mihiel and the Meuse-Argonne in 1917 and 1918. Unfortunately, since the editors chose to format the history in huge **Adobe Acrobat** files, these texts can be awkward to search and use effectively, especially when trying to reproduce some of the excellent maps and photographs available here. Fascinated by military history, students will discover the value and excitement of reading primary sources and integrating information from various people to make sense of America's military role in the "War to Make the World Safe for Democracy."

The American Civil War and CD-ROMs

Every time scholars think popular interest in the history of the American Civil War of 1861-1865 may be about to wane, something occurs to revive public curiosity. In the wake of filmmaker Ken Burn's "The Civil War" documentary which aired on public television stations in 1990, millions of Americans wanted to learn more about this central event in nineteenth-century American history. Not surprisingly, many CDs about the Civil War have appeared from computer games to photographic collections to serious scholarly studies.

Until relatively recently, historians often focused on the military history of the Civil War to study the role of generals, armies, navies, politicians, diplomats, and new weapons technologies on Civil War battlefields. The standard historical source for these studies was the *Official Records of the War of the Rebellion*, (1880-1901) a 128-volume compilation of after-action reports by Union military commanders written somewhere between weeks to several months after battles to describe the tactical role of regiments, divisions, corps, and armies in specific battles and campaigns. Two commercial publishers raced against each other to print **CD-ROM** versions of this collection that costs hundreds of dollars in modern reprinted clothbound editions, but only about $70 in **CD-ROM** format. The Guild Press of Indiana lost the race, but produced a superior product with an effective **search engine** that allows for name, place, keyword, and unit searches through all 128 volumes in seconds to locate primary sources that students can use to write papers on leaders, units, battles, and campaigns. A bookmarking function allows users to save records for use in research projects. In the original 1996 **CD-ROM** edition, Guild Press editors included guides to the original series, a modern guide to the original index, and a standard reference work on *Regimental Losses in the American Civil War*.

Teachers need to be aware that more recent investigations centering on social, cultural, women's and southern history are not reflected in this more traditional source first published amidst the nostalgic romanticization of the war. Recognizing the popularity of

Civil War studies, Guild Press followed up this well executed CD version of the *Official Records* with succeeding CDs on *The Civil War CD-ROM II: Official Records of the Union and Confederate Navies in the War of the Rebellion*, *Atlas of the Official Record of the Civil War*, *Confederate Military History*, the *Southern Historical Society Papers*, and *Campaigns of the Civil War and the Navy in the Civil War* for prices ranging from $40 to $70. More recently, the press published the *Complete Civil War on DVD* that includes all these CDs and the capability to search all in one search. We can anticipate many more entries into the field of Civil War history, including **multimedia** games available for sale in stores in almost every community in the United States.

The highly innovative "Valley of the Shadow: Two Communities in the American Civil War" project directed by Edward L. Ayers at the University of Virginia is often cited as the most in-depth, sophisticated history Web site currently online. Ayers and his very talented staff of graduate student researchers led by Anne S. Rubin of the Institute for Advanced Technology in the Humanities at the University of Virginia have now made one part of this vast project accessible in **CD-ROM** format as *The Eve of War: Valley of the Shadow, Two Communities in the American Civil War* (New York: W.W. Norton, 2000) along with an accompanying 103-page book for use by students either in the classroom or for class assignments. Sources from the Web site database include newspapers, diaries and letters, music, images, census and tax records, church records, and enlistment records at the start of the war. Part one of a projected three-part **CD-ROM** series, this work challenges students to use the 1859-1861 portion of the Web site database to ask questions about the political, social, and community roots of the war, while promising to raise more questions about the course and consequences of the war in the second and third parts to come. Teachers can use the CD to compare the editorial direction of the project and its implicit historical interpretation with analyses conducted by students using the same sources. One can hardly ask for a more exciting way to teach students about historical methods. After detailing some criticisms of how the **CD-ROM** is both different from and similar to the much larger Web site, historian Thomas J. Brown in an important review highlights its significance not only as a tool to empower students but also as creative scholarship in its own right:

Valley of the Shadow represents a milestone in American historiography. A digital archive that demonstrates new modes of accessing information and an interactive tool that fosters learning in classrooms and other settings, it makes advances in two of the areas that have dominated efforts to apply recent technology to the study of history. Most important, *Valley of the Shadow* combines its reference and pedagogical missions with the presentation of original historical scholarship. ("The House Divided and Digitized," *Reviews in American History* 29 (June 2001): 213.)

We sometimes forget that historical research involves cooperative efforts among many people who bring research projects to fruition. Ayers and his staff work closely with members of the Virginia Center for Digital History including director William G. Thomas and former associate director Alice E. Carter (now project manager for the **New York Times** on the Web). Thomas and Carter have co-edited an extremely useful work, *The Civil War on the Web: A Guide to the Very Best Sites* (Wilmington, DE: Scholarly Resources, 2001). Drawing on their experience with the Valley of the Shadow Project, Thomas and Carter provide a thoughtful introduction and user's guide, review and rate major sites dedicated to the history of the Civil War, and catalog the selected sites by category. Significantly, the organization of this work reflects recent trends in Civil War history moving beyond military, political, and diplomatic history to encompass social, women's, African American, and the history of ordinary soldiers on both sides. In a revealing editorial choice, Scholarly Resources also includes a **CD-ROM** version of the work in **Adobe Acrobat file format**. Students can use either the printed book or the Acrobat file to access the volume's contents, clicking on hot links to the Web sites reviewed and rated by the editors.

Publishers have begun experimenting with multi-format versions of works that can be used as traditional text, **hypertext**, and **multimedia** versions that both students and teachers of all ages and levels of computer literacy can be comfortable working with. No doubt scholars and publishers will be bringing out more such experimental works in the near future that will blur the lines between print, **hypertext**, and fully interactive forms of history. Teachers will need to familiarize themselves with at least some of these new ways of presenting the past in ways that younger students will find attractive and worth their time and energy.

History Textbooks and More on CD-ROM

Recognizing the computer and **digital** literacy of today's students, an increasing number of publishers now bring out both printed and **CD-ROM** versions of textbooks for use in United States history, Western Civilization, and World History survey courses. Yet the nature, scope, and quality of the historical materials in these **CD-ROMs** varies from publisher to publisher and text to text. One of the earliest and highest quality **CD-ROM** textbooks emerged from the innovative work of the American Social History Project (http://www.ashp.cuny.edu/) that focused on presenting the findings of the new social history of the U.S. in college classrooms. Going beyond another version of the traditional printed textbook in the medium of the **CD-ROM**, the project brings **multimedia** materials to bear in the study and teaching of U.S. history.

Roy Rosenzweig, Steve Brier, and Josh Brown, three of the early members of the project, labored intently to produce one of the first truly **multimedia** history texts keeping in mind the primary focus of the classroom. ***Who Built America? From the Centennial Celebration of 1876 to the Great War of 1914 CD-ROM*** incorporates sights, sounds, and texts in a way that brings history alive for students and teachers alike. Starting from the first edition of the award-winning U.S. history text, ***Who Built America?*** (1989, 1992), the authors bring together several thousand pages of text, hundreds of pictures, sixty graphs and charts, four hours of audio, and forty-five minutes of film in an easy-to-use interface that anyone who can use a computer mouse can navigate within minutes of a painless installation process. In addition to including all of the printed text, the **CD-ROM** provides links to revealing oral history interviews, contemporary music, speeches of the day, and movie clips at the birth of the motion picture industry. While the disc uses such traditional elements as U.S. and world maps, timelines, and chapter bibliographies of recent histories, it also provides interactivity between sources and students. Design of the CD allows cut and paste editing for note taking, use of direct quotations, and creation of customized resource collections that let students build interpretive projects of their own. The timeline function provides for comparison of the work's main themes of world events, politics, the economy, society, culture, births and deaths in a given year, and an overview bringing these together in one place. While this project does present a strong interpretive focus from the new social history of African Americans, immigrants, women, and workers, it simultaneously shows students how their teachers and other historians use sources to build historical interpretations—how information becomes transformed into knowledge. This textbook and its **CD-ROM** version were received so enthusiastically that the American Social History Project issued a revised edition of the original two-volume text and a successor **CD-ROM**, ***Who Built America? CD-ROM: From the Centennial Celebration of 1876 to the Great War of 1914 to the Dawn of the Atomic Age in 1946*** in 2000 just in time for the 21st century.

Documents, Images, Sounds, and Interpretation

As students and teachers become more adept at using new kinds of computer and instructional technology, they will find companies responding to their interest in new forms of history. **CD-ROMs** make interactive, **multimedia** history possible in ways that can enhance the learning of individual students and engender excitement about historical study. Unfortunately, many history **CD-ROMs** currently available are not well planned, edited, and compiled. One of the few exceptions can be found in a multi-volume series, ***American Journey: History in Your Hands*** produced by Primary Source Microform, now a division of the Gale Group, a well-respected publisher of reference works widely used by the library community. To date, the series includes titles dealing with the social history of African Americans, Asian Americans, Hispanic Americans, immigrants, Native Americans, and women. Topical works deal with the Constitution and the Supreme Court and civil rights, while chronologically focused works explore the history of the American Revolution, the Civil War, Westward Expansion, the Great Depression and the New Deal, the Cold War, and the Vietnam Era. The editorial staff directed by Bennett Lovett-Graff wisely chose to publish each volume both as a **CD-ROM** for use by individual students and teachers and on a subscription basis in the form of a password-accessible Web site (http://www.americanjourney.psmedia.com/) for institutional use. Prominent scholars specializing in the area under study are selected to serve as general editor of a volume, then additional scholars may be asked to contribute sections to the project.

As the general editor and author of most of the text for **American Journey: World War I and the Jazz Age** (2000), this author participated in the process of outlining the structure of the work, compiling lists of primary source documents and photographs, selecting contemporary speeches and newsreel clips, and using sheet music to record popular music of the period. The challenge was to show students complete text of primary source documents, original black and white photographs along with color posters, and clips of speeches and newsreel footage without editorially "cleaning up" these sources for modern consumption. This **multimedia** history of the United States from 1890 to 1929 presents both an interpretive line and a detailed narrative of Progressive reform, U.S. intervention in World War I, and the economic, social, and cultural events of the 1920s. Integrating social, economic, labor, women's, African American, political, military, and diplomatic history, the work includes over two hundred primary source documents with individual head notes, seventeen interpretive essays, over three hundred images with separate captions, popular period music, video clips with the original narration, bibliographies for further reading, an annotated, interactive timeline, and multiple search functions. Interpretive essays employ **hypertext** to link students to pictures of historical actors, copies of documents under discussion, headnotes and captions to place each source in historical context, and links among and between documents, sights, and sounds so that students can observe and study how the historical art of interpretation is practiced. The timeline, bibliographies, and multiple search functions allow students to research specific time periods, topics, and people while showing the significance of different kinds of history and the need for intellectual synthesis of sources from a variety of formats and venues. Each section refers students to some of the best Web sites currently online for that subject.

CD-ROMs as Multimedia History

In a 1995 article, "'So, What's Next for Clio?' CD-ROM and Historians," in the *Journal of American History* (For an online version, see http://chnm.gmu.edu/chnm/clio.html), Roy Rosenzweig pointed out that **CD-ROMs** can be used as historical databases, documentaries, games, and books. He reminds us to be careful about assuming that the use of new technology will necessarily lead to good, high-quality history. Taken for what they can offer to students and teachers, **CD-ROMs** can serve as valuable tools. They allow for the collection, storage, organization, and analysis of large amounts of primary source materials not only in the traditional text document form, but also in more modern **multimedia** form. Graphical images of drawings, paintings, posters, black and white photographs, color photos, film clips, and, theoretically, full motion pictures bring light and depth to history. Sounds enliven history, excite students, and challenge teachers to present history in all its complex fascination with people in the past. With the arrival of **multimedia** history, we now face a future brimming with the potential of bringing together documents, sights, and sounds for a rich, full-fledged, multi-dimensional kind of history made possible with new technology. Whether that dream becomes a reality is largely up to us and what we do in the classrooms of the near future.

9. IS DIGITAL HISTORY MORE THAN THE SUM OF ITS PARTS?

Learning and using the capability of the **Internet** and new technology such as **CD-ROM**'s to transform text, images, and sounds into binary digits expands our intellectual power to organize, transmit, share, and search information. Remember that more data does not automatically translate into better history, science, art, literature, music, business or any other human construction. Only the human experience of creating and synthesizing can turn information into knowledge or binary digits into something more beautiful or enlightening than the mere sum of their electrical parts.

We have explored the many ways the **Internet** enhances historical understanding:

As an archive of primary sources.

As a **multimedia** gallery of text, audio and still and moving images.

As an expanded learning space.

As a **search engine** of historical inquiry.

As a simulator of historical events.

As a medium of social interaction and historical collaboration.

As **hypertext** trails of historical knowledge.

As **multimedia** history along with **CD-ROM**s.

As a useful learning tool for students and teachers.

The **Internet** can serve as a magnificent tool; however, only the students, teachers and scholars who use it to reconstruct and give meaning to the past can make it yield lively, artful history worthy of our craft pride. Technology may and hopefully will serve as a powerful means to effect revealing historical knowledge in the lives of those willing to see the future potential of the **Internet** to understand the human past.

10. PROFESSIONAL HISTORIANS AND THE INTERNET

When **ARPANET** started in the late 1960s, scientists were the most common users of this primitive collection of computers that later became the worldwide network we now know as the **Internet**. Not surprisingly, scientists discovered how to take advantage of the Net more quickly than humanists or social scientists. While that began to change in the 1990s, historians learned to use the **Internet** more slowly than colleagues in many other academic disciplines. As teachers, researchers, readers, and authors, we expect many things in light of the almost utopian visions caste about in the wake of the emergence of the personal computer, **e-mail**, and the **World Wide Web**. Let's take a careful look at how various part of this vast information resource might help us to do our jobs in the classroom, the library, the archive, the office, and the broader historical profession.

The vast majority of historians in the United States work at community colleges, colleges, and four-year universities where teaching is the most important part of our daily lives. Appropriately, classroom teaching will change along with new kinds of instructional technology such as the personal computer connected to the **Internet**, **CD-ROMs**, and what may be a profusion of devices in the future such as wireless **PDAs (personal digital assistants)**, cell phones, and, some predict, computer-like technology that attaches to or is part of our clothing. Development of educational and teaching-oriented Web sites has become ubiquitous with many younger, technologically experienced teachers creating online course Web pages and specialized Web sites for use in the classroom. One of the earliest professional groups in the humanities to experiment with teaching innovations over the **Internet** is the American Studies Association that built the extensive and theoretically sophisticated American Studies Crossroads Project site at Georgetown University (http://www.georgetown.edu/crossroads/). Under the direction of Randy Bass, this project has evolved into an extensive Web of resources and thoughtful online materials that historians can use as a model worthy of emulation. Bass' own work in the use of **hypertext** to teach American Studies led to *Engines of Inquiry: A Practical Guide for Using Technology to Teach American*

Culture accessible online at http://www.georgetown.edu/crossroads/guide/guide.html. Rumor has it that a new edition of this valuable work will soon be available.

Inspired by the work of working-class historian Herbert Gutman, participants in the American Social History Project (http://www.ashp.cuny.edu/) became the first group of historians who seriously investigated and experimented in **multimedia** classroom technology through the production of historical documentaries and the social history-centered U.S. history text, ***Who Built America: Working People and the Nation's Economy, Politics, Culture, and Society***, first published in 1989, then in a revised edition in 2000. Having developed expertise in the design, use, and distribution of new classroom materials such as the first ***Who Built America CD-ROM*** (1993), such people as Stephen Brier, Josh Brown, and Roy Rosenzweig helped to expand this project, now housed at the Graduate Center of the City University of New York along with the Center for Media and Learning. Cooperating with the Crossroads Project, the American Social History Project later received funds from the National Endowment for the Humanities to create a series of regional centers to share the results of work done by the New Media Classroom (http://www.ashp.cuny.edu/index_new.html). Located at Washington State University (Pullman, WA), Cerritos College (Los Angeles, CA), Mott Community College (Flint, MI), Pembroke Hill School (Kansas City, MO), Vanderbilt University (Nashville, TN), Millersville University (Millersville, PA), the Borough of Manhattan Community College (New York, NY), and Assumption College (Worcester, MA), these regional centers created week-long institutes to train teachers in the use of new classroom technologies using Bass's ***Engines of Inquiry*** as a kind of handbook. Under Pennee Bender, Joshua Brown, Manding Darboe, Donna Thompson, and Andrea Ades Vasquez of the New Media Classroom project staff, veterans of these early seminars created classroom resources, including a series of practical exercises for teacher use (http://www.ashp.cuny.edu/nmcresources.shtml), and the ***New Media Classroom Teacher's Handbook*** *(2000)*, now used in the summertime seminars to spark interest and enthusiasm in the use of collaborative writing, classroom software writing programs such as WebBoard (http://www.webboard.com/) or **WebCT** (http://www.webct.com/), **multimedia** resources on the **Internet**, student-designed and built Web projects, and some of the best history-oriented Web sites. This joint effort to help teachers across the United States become aware of new teaching methods and technologies continues to grow through a new effort, Learning to Look: Visual Resources and the U.S. Past in the New Media Classroom (http://www.ashp.cuny.edu/nmcprograms.shtml) in cooperation with The Visible Knowledge Project: Learning/ Technology/Inquiry (http://crossroads.georgetown.edu/ vkp/). Both projects intend to get teachers thinking about the concept of "visual literacy" as a way to help students learn the fundamentals and application of critical thinking and learning about non-text based source materials.

Roy Rosenzweig, a longtime activist in the American Social History Project, now serves as the director of the Center for History and the New Media (http://chnm.gmu.edu/) at George Mason University that recently began a new program emphasis in New Media and New Technology and Public and Applied History. That center operates a superb Web site, History Matters, (http://historymatters.gmu.edu/), showcasing model online syllabi, primary documents, a constantly updated database of history Web sites, an archive of Web-based classroom projects, and samples of student Web work that new, mid-career, and experienced teachers can draw from and add to.

Perhaps the most extensive network of teachers and scholars centers around the H-Net: Humanities & Social Sciences OnLine (http://www2.h-net.msu.edu/) community consisting of hundreds of volunteer list editors, book review editors, and Web site editors who work with the small, highly dedicated staff in the Matrix Center at Michigan State University. Begun under the energetic initiative of people like Bill Cecil-Fronsman, Richard Jensen, Peter Knupfer, Mark Kornbluh, Jim Oberly, Wendy Plotkin, and Gus Seligman, H-Net has grown continuously from an initially small group of specialized mailing lists into the most important set of scholarly networks among historians and other humanists and social scientists on the **Internet**. In 1997, the American Historical Association recognized the significance of H-Netters by awarding H-Net the James Harvey Robinson Prize for a teaching aid. Teachers and scholars can join multiple networks, listen and read postings as "lurkers," and actively participate in civil, high quality discussions about teaching, research, and the use of new instructional technology. H-Net regularly redesigns its Web site to meet the changing needs of members, archiving posts, book reviews, and resources in specialized areas on individual list Web sites.

As **Internet** usage has permeated the broader culture, both individual historians and small groups of like-minded scholars have learned to use the **Internet** to advance their work. While historians at less well-recognized and funded public universities and teaching-oriented liberal arts colleges created some of the earliest and highest quality Web sites, by 2000 most history departments had some kind of Web site. The Center for History and New Media provides an updated listing of History Departments Around the World (http://history.gmu.edu/scripts/departments.php) for scholars who wish to contact other historians around the world. Independent historians not connected with a particular institution and adjunct faculty can network through the National Coalition for Independent Scholars (http://www.ncis.org/) and the National Adjunct Faculty Guild (http://www.adjunctadvocate.com/).

While advising students about historical essays based on secondary sources and research papers, you can use the extensive collection of online library catalogs and archival guides for manuscript collections. You might begin with the sites that librarians use, such as the Internet Public Library, LibDex, and LibWeb, then check the online catalogs of such major research libraries as the Library of Congress, The British Library, the New York and Chicago Public Libraries. A variety of other libraries and archives around the world now make the catalogs and manuscript inventories accessible online research papers, you can use the extensive collection of online library catalogs and archival guides for manuscript collections. You might begin with the sites that librarians use, such as the Internet Public Library, LibDex, and LibWeb, then check the online catalogs of such major research libraries as the Library of Congress, The British Library, and the New York and Chicago Public Libraries. A variety of other libraries and archives around the world now make the catalogs and manuscript inventories accessible online at the sites listed at the end of this work under **Libraries and Archives.**

Every month historical journals appear online using several models: free access, free and pay for service sites, and subscription-only services. Following a 1997 conference, editors of the journals of the American Historical Association and the Organization of American Historians sponsored creation of The History Cooperative where members of these and other professional groups can find sophisticated online versions of the *American Historical Review*, the *Journal of American History*, *The History Teacher*, the *Law and History Review*, the *Western Historical Quarterly*, and the *William and Mary Quarterly*. The near future will see plenty of experimentation by publishers, editors, professional groups, and individuals in the rapidly changing world of online publishing. Early efforts on these lines include the History E-Book Project led by the American Council of Learned Societies and the netLibrary that brings together academic and commercial publishers, libraries and schools, editors and researchers, and writers and their readers. Resources for online journals, manuscript inventories, and the future of e-texts are listed below.

Journals, Manuscripts, and the Electronic Future

History Journals Guide (WWW-Virtual Library, Stefan Blaschke)
http://www.history-journals.de/

National Union Catalog of Manuscript Collections [NUCMC] (Library of Congress)
http://lcweb.loc.gov/coll/nucmc/

Archival and Manuscript Repositories in the United States (Library of Congress)
http://lcweb.loc.gov/coll/nucmc/other.html

Repositories of Primary Sources (University of Idaho)
http://www.uidaho.edu/special-collections/Other.Repositories.html

History Journals and the Electronic Future:
The final report of a conference held at
Indiana University, Bloomington, August 3-8, 1997
http://www.indiana.edu/~ahr/report.htm

The History Cooperative
http://www.historycooperative.org/

The History E-Book Project (American Council of Learned
Societies)
http://www.historyebook.org/

netLibrary
http://www.netlibrary.com/

Professional organizations for historians now place valuable
information about membership, publications, newsletters,
activities, announcements, conventions, meeting programs,
reviews, and other materials online. The American Historical
Association (http://www.theaha.org/), the Organization of
American Historians (http://www.oah.org/), and The Historical
Society (http://www.bu.edu/historic/) have Web sites as do many
more specialized associations that you can use to find addresses,
telephone numbers, and **e-mail** addresses for friends, colleagues,
and researchers interested in the same topics you are. Graduate
students employ these online resources very astutely today to
network, find out information about prospective employers, and
save money, time, and energy on research trips and making
contacts with practicing historians. It would not be surprising to
see elementary and secondary school history teachers turning to
e-mail, Web sites, and online publication of lesson plans and
course design in collaboration with teachers in community
colleges, four-year colleges and universities, and research
universities in the near future. As historians become more familiar
and comfortable with the **Internet** and new instructional
technologies, these tools will serve as the newest addition to the
combination of skills that make the historian's craft an ever-
changing mosaic stretching from the distant past into the present
and off into the future.

APPENDIX

Glossary

Adobe Acrobat. Software program developed by Adobe to allow for presentation of files and images across various computer platforms, operating systems (Windows, Macintosh, Unix, and Linux), and programs preserving the original formatting for bold face, italics, special characters, and other features. Use of the free Adobe Acrobat Reader (http://www.adobe.com/) allows users to use a standard **file format** on many different kinds of computers.

ARPANET. The Advanced Research Project Agency Network founded in 1969 to advance communication among research scientists, the U.S. military, and government agencies in the event of a nuclear war during the late Cold War years to decentralize the impact of destruction of information in the wake of a nuclear conflict.

BlackBoard. Commercial software program used by many institutions to help teachers integrate writing, computer, **e-mail**, and **Internet** research skills in the classroom. For information, see http://www.blackboard.com/.

Bookmark. A marker that allows you to save a Web address on **Netscape Navigator** so that you can return to it later. Called a **Favorite** on **Microsoft Internet Explorer** or a Hotlist on some other **browsers**.

Browser. A software application that translates **HTML** files into text, sounds and images so that you can view them on the **World Wide Web** by pointing and clicking your computer mouse.

Cable Modem. A hardware device allowing subscribers to use cable television or telephone lines to achieve faster **Internet** connections that will become increasingly more useful and expected as **Internet** sites employ sound file, music, and streaming video.

CD-ROM. An acronym that stands for **Compact Disc – Read Only Memory**. CD-ROMs and newer DVD-ROMs can store vast amounts of digitized information, reproducing it as text, sound and images on your computer screen or a DVD player.

CERN. The **Conseil Européene pour la Recherche Nucléaire [European Organization for Nuclear Research] (CERN)** outside Geneva, Switzerland where physicist Tim Berners-Lee first developed a **graphical user interface** that later was developed further into the **Internet** browser software commercialized by Microsoft Corporation and Netscape Communcations as the and **Internet Explorer** and **Netscape Navigator.**

Digital. Value represented in binary digits, 1s and 0s.

Domain. The general category that identifies a computer providing **Internet** services (e.g. edu for education, com for commercial, gov for government, org for nonprofit, etc.).

DSL. **Digital subscriber line** connection offered by some telephone and cable television companies to individuals and small businesses as a faster (varying speeds almost up to the speed of a **T-1** line) connection than a dial-up **modem** link, but slower than a **T-1** connection. It provides a good compromise between cost and speed for individual **Internet** users at home when a faster institutional connection is not available.

E-mail. Electronic mail transmitted on the **Internet** or a local computer network.

Emoticons. Symbols used by authors of **e-mail** to indicate emotional intent to avoid misunderstanding or misinterpretation of text messages. For example, :-) indicates the author is smiling and intends the comment to be read as humorous or joking. For a good sampling, see http://www.computeruser.com/resources/dictionary/emoticons.html.

ENIAC. The **Electronic Numerical Integrator and Calculator**, located at the University of Pennsylvania, was one of the earliest computers used by the U.S. Army for military purposes in the immediate post-World War II years.

Favorite. A marker that allows you to save a Web address on **Microsoft Internet Explorer.**

File formats. Digital materials come in a variety of formats such as text, rtf word processing files, **html**, and **sgml** for text-oriented documents; **bmp, gif, jpeg, tiff, and bmp** for pictures; **wav, MP3, and ra** for sounds and music; and **mpeg, QuickTime, RealMedia**, and **Windows Media** for audiovisual clips and motion pictures. New **file formats** emerge constantly in the wake of new hardware and software applications coming online.

FTP. File Transfer Protocol, a method of transferring files via the **Internet** from one computer to another.

Gopher. An early method of storing and accessing textual data before the **World Wide Web** that allowed **Internet** users to dig and tunnel for information though a series of hierarchically structured menus and sub-menus.

GUI. Graphical User Interface, now common to all Macintosh and Windows operating systems, enables computer users to select commands, programs and files by pointing and clicking icons, pull-down menus, scroll bars and dialog boxes.

Home Page. The starting or gateway page of any Web site.

HTML. Hypertext Markup Language, the protocol used to write **World Wide Web** pages.

HTTP. Hypertext Transfer Protocol, the standard for managing communication between **World Wide Web** links.

Hyperlink. Any text or image on a Web page which connects, by pointing and clicking the computer mouse, to another location in the same Web document or to another Web page.

Hypermedia. Multimedia **hypertext** links in graphics, text, sound, animation and video common to the **World Wide Web**, **CD-ROMs** and other software applications.

Hypertext. A method of organizing knowledge by association rather than linear sequence. **Hypertext** is used by the **World Wide Web**, **CD-ROMs** and some other software applications to create links and paths of knowledge from text to text and document to document.

Internet. A global system linking networks of computers and resources (e.g. **World Wide Web**, **e-mail**, **FTP**, **gophers**, etc.) in more than 200 countries.

ISDN. Integrated Services Digital Network allows for fast (16-64k bytes per second) transmission of voice, video, and data information in **digital** format. Offered by telephone companies to individual residential users, **ISDN** makes for a faster connection than dial-up (14-56k bytes per second) **modem** links and will become more common in the next decade as prices for this service come down.

ISP. An **Internet** Service Provider sells **Internet** access to schools, government agencies, private businesses, and individual residential customers. Major **ISPs** would include America On Line (AOL), AT&T WorldNet, and Earthlink.

Java. A programming language designed to run on almost any computer platform (Macintosh, Unix, Windows, etc.) and used primarily to add animation to **World Wide Web** pages. **Java** applets allow Web sites designers to add **multimedia** capabilities to their sites without loading large software programs onto users' computers. Eventually **Java** programming will be used on many electronic devices and appliances in homes, businesses, schools, and government agencies.

Listserv, listproc, or majordomo. Software programs that automatically send **e-mail** to everyone who subscribes to and posts messages on an electronic discussion forum.

Microsoft Internet Explorer. The **Internet browser** developed by Microsoft Corporation as part of the Windows operating system which competed successfully with **Netscape Navigator** to become the most widely used browser software by 2000. Legal challenges by the federal government may lead to separation of the browser and operating system software programs at some point in the future.

Modem. A device that enables computers to transmit information to one another via telephone lines.

MOO/MUD. **MUD's** (Multi-User Dungeon) and **MOO's** (MUD Object Oriented), virtual environments that can be used for scholarly exploration, simulation and communication.

Mosaic. The original graphical user interface (**gui**), or **browser**, designed in 1992 by computer scientists at the National Center for Supercomputing Applications center at the University of Illinois at Urbana-Champaign that allowed for use of graphics as well as text on the **Internet**. **Mosiac** served as the core and predecessor for the two most commonly used **Internet browsers**, **Microsoft Internet Explorer** and **Netscape Navigator**.

Multimedia. Computer technology that presents information using a combination of text, audio and visual elements.

Netscape Navigator/Communicator. One of two commonly use **Internet** browsers used by millions of people to access **Internet** sites. Navigator is the browser, while Communicator is the entire package which includes an **e-mail** program and a simple Web site editing application. Once an independent company, it is now part of America On Line (AOL), a major **Internet service provider**.

Newsgroups. Single-topic, electronic discussion groups that are part of a worldwide network called **Usenet**.

PDAs. **Personal Digital Assistants** serve as small, hand-held devices that provide users with capabilities of arranging personal calendars, taking notes, and storing telephone numbers, and **e-mail** addresses. Sophisticated, wireless versions allow access to the **e-mail** and the **Internet** for travelers, researchers, and business people. Wireless telephones and PDAs will soon become commonly used devices to read e-mail and access the Web.

Plug-ins. Programs that can be added to a Web **browser** to enhance its power.

QuickTime. Apple Computer developed this innovative software program to create and display sophisticated sound and video files across computer platforms such as Macintosh and Windows-based computers to serve as the industry standard for audiovisual multimedia software.

RAND Corporation. The Research and Development Corporation organized as a think tank for operations research for the United States Air Force during the early years of the Cold War that helped to pioneer the idea for the original computer network that later became the **Internet**.

RealPlayer or audio plug-in. A software application in both standalone and plugin with browser versions allowing the user to listen to or view sound, music, video, and motion picture files available in both free and commercial versions from Real.com.

Search Engine(s). **Internet** sites devoted to running programs that regularly travel the **Internet** seeking and cataloging files, directories within sites, and entire Web sites based on predetermined subject categories and keywords that can later be checked by users looking for particular information. They serve as a kind of ongoing set of directories or indexes for the **Internet**, but these sites catalog only a very small percentage of active sites at any one point in time and can become out of date very quickly.

Server. A networked computer that provides services and/or information.

Shockwave. Macromedia developed Director **Shockwave** Studio software that allows Web editors to combine animated images, audio, and video content and to develop innovative graphical design sites. **Internet** users can download the **Shockwave** player for free to display this content.

"Snail Mail." Term used by experienced **Internet** users for traditional written or printed letters sent through the mail service rather than electronically via **e-mail**.

T-1, T-3 lines. Extremely fast point-to-point, long distance computer connections which expedite much speedier and higher quality links than possible by **modem** to the **World Wide Web**.

TCP/IP. Transmission Control Protocol/Internet Protocol, a uniform standard for point-to-point communication on the **Internet** by computers using different operating systems (Macintosh, Windows, UNIX).

Telnet. A protocol that allows the user to log into and use the files of another computer on the **Internet**, including online library catalogues.

URL. Uniform Resource Locator, a protocol for **World Wide Web** addresses.

Usenet. A contraction for User Network, a worldwide list of single-issue, electronic discussion **newsgroups**.

WebCT. Commercial software program used by many institutions to help teachers integrate writing, computer, **e-mail**, and **Internet** research skills in the classroom. For information, see http://www.webct.com/.

Windows Media Player. A software application in both standalone and **plug-in** with browser versions allowing the user to listen to or view sound, music, video, and motion picture files available in both free and commercial versions from Microsoft Corporation. Newer versions of the Microsoft Windows operating system come with this program already installed.

World Wide Web. A global system of **hypermedia** pages on the **Internet**.

Zip Drive. A built-in or external device allowing for storage of 100 or 250 megabytes of information on a disk rather than the traditional 1.44 megabytes on a floppy diskette.

Internet Sites Mentioned in This Work (in the order cited above):

Tennessee Tech History Web Site
(Patrick D. Reagan, Tennessee Technological University)
http://www2.tntech.edu/history/

The Victorian Web
(George P. Landow, Brown University)
http://www.victorianweb.org/

WWW VL [Virtual Library] History Central Catalogue
(Lynn Nelson, University of Kansas)
http://www.ku.edu/history/VL/

Don Mabry's Historical Text Archive
http://historicaltextarchive.com/

American Memory: Historical Collections from the National Digital Library
(Library of Congress)
http://memory.loc.gov/

Valley of the Shadow: Two Communities in the American Civil War
(Edward L. Ayers, Anne S. Rubin, William G. Thomas, III, University of Virginia)
http://jefferson.village.virginia.edu/vshadow2/

The Labyrinth: Resources for Medieval Studies
http://labyrinth.georgetown.edu/

Chicago Historical Society
http://www.chicagohs.org/

Nagasaki Journey
http://www.exploratorium.edu/nagasaki/mainn.html

Crisis at Fort Sumter (Richard B. Latner, Tulane University)
http://www.tulane.edu/~latner/

The Red Hot Jazz Archive
http://www.redhotjazz.com/
The Foundation Course in African Dance Drumming
(C. K. Ladzekpo, University of California, Berkeley)
http://www.cnmat.berkeley.edu/~ladzekpo/Foundation.html

Bobby Sanabria jazz site
http://www.jazzcorner.com/sanabria/sanabriahome.html

National Museum of African Art (Smithsonian Institution)
http://www.nmafa.si.edu/

Art Museum Network
http://www.amn.org/

H-Net: Humanities & Social Sciences OnLine
http://www2.h-net.msu.edu/

The Visible Knowledge Project: Learning/Technology/Inquiry
http://crossroads.georgetown.edu/vkp/

The List: The Definitive ISP Buyer's Guide
http://thelist.internet.com/

WebCT
http://www.webct.com/

BlackBoard
http://www.blackboard.com/

Emoticons (Computer User High Tech Dictionary)
http://www.computeruser.com/resources/dictionary/
emoticons.html

Discussion Groups: Mailing Lists (Library of Congress)
http://www.loc.gov/loc/guides/maillist.html

Internet & Networking: Internet Mailing Lists Guides and
Resources
(International Federation of Library Associations and Institutions)
http://www.ifla.org/I/training/listserv/lists.htm

CataList: The Official Catalog of LISTSERV Lists (L-Soft)
http://www.lsoft.com/catalist.html

Google Groups (Google.com)
http://groups.google.com/

Liszts: Directory of E-Mail Discussion Groups
http://www.liszts.com/

PAML: Publicly Accessible Mailing Lists (Neosoft)
http://paml.net/

Tile.Net/Newsgroup
http://www.tile.net/news/

Discussion Groups: Usenet Newsgroups (Library of Congress)
http://www.loc.gov/loc/guides/news.html

Soc.History.War.Vietnam Newsgroup Files
(Vietnam War Internet Project)
http://www.lbjlib.utexas.edu/shwv/shwv-top.html

H-Net: Humanities & Social Sciences OnLine
http://www2.h-net.msu.edu/

H-Net Teaching
http://www2.h-net.msu.edu/teaching/

H-Net Discussion Networks
http://www2.h-net.msu.edu/lists/

H-LatAm
http://www2.h-net.msu.edu/~latam/

H-SHGAPE
http://www2.h-net.msu.edu/~shgape/

H-Net Reviews in the Humanities and Social Sciences
http://www2.h-net.msu.edu/reviews/

H-Net Job Guide for the Humanities and Social Sciences
http://www2.h-net.msu.edu/jobs/

Locating Information on the Internet (Library of Congress)
http://www.loc.gov/loc/guides/locate.html

Yahoo search
http://www.yahoo.com/

Alta Vista search
http://www.altavista.com/

Excite search engine
http://www.excite.com/

Google search engine
http://www.google.com/

Northern Light search engine
http://www.northernlight.com/

Search Engine Watch
http://www.searchenginewatch.com/

Father Ryan's Holocaust Class
(Father Ryan High School, Nashville, Tennessee)
http://www.fatherryan.org/frhsonline/foreman/

Today in History (American Memory, Library of Congress)
http://lcweb2.loc.gov/ammem/today/today.html

Today in History (News from AP/New York Times)
http://www.nytimes.com/aponline/national/AP-History.html

On This Day (New York Times)
http://www.nytimes.com/learning/general/onthisday/index.html

American National Biography (Oxford University Press)
http://www.anb.org/

Biography.com (Arts & Entertainment Network)
http://www.biography.com/

The Historian's Sources (Learning Page, Library of Congress)
http://lcweb2.loc.gov/learn/lessons/psources/pshome.html

Repositories of Primary Sources (University of Idaho)
http://www.uidaho.edu/special-collections/Other.Repositories.html

Reading About the World: A Reader for the Study of World Civilizations
http://www.wsu.edu:8080/~wldciv/world_civ_reader/

World History Archives
http://www.hartford-hwp.com/archives/index.html

World History (Tennessee Technological University)
http://www2.tntech.edu/history/world.html

EuroDocs: Primary Historical Documents from Western Europe (Brigham Young University)
http://www.lib.byu.edu/~rdh/eurodocs/index.html

Avalon Project: Documents in Law, History and Diplomacy (Yale Law School)
http://www.yale.edu/lawweb/avalon/avalon.htm

Making of America (University of Michigan)
http://moa.umdl.umich.edu/)

Chronology of U.S. Historical Documents (University of Oklahoma College of Law)
http://www.law.ou.edu/hist/

Electronic Text Center (University of Virginia)
http://etext.lib.virginia.edu/uvaonline.html

Project Gutenberg
http://www.gutenberg.net/

Online Books Page
http://digital.library.upenn.edu/books/

Library Catalogs and Archives
(Tennessee Technological University History Web site)
http://www2.tntech.edu/history/libs.html

LibDex: The Library Index
http://www.libdex.com/

Gabriel: Gateway to Europe's National Libraries
http://portico.bl.uk/gabriel/en/countries.html

Online Library Card Catalogs in Asia
(East Asian Library, University of Pittsburgh)
http://www.pitt.edu/%7Eealib/libcat.htm

National Gallery of the Spoken Word (Michigan State University)
http://www.ngsw.org/

Vincent Voice Library (Michigan State University)
http://www.lib.msu.edu/vincent/

History and Politics Out Loud
http://www.hpol.org/

National Sound Archive (British Library)
http://www.bl.uk/collections/sound-archive/cat.html

Rock & Roll Hall of Fame and Museum (Cleveland, OH)
http://www.rockhall.com/

Corbis (includes the old Bettman Archive photographs)
http://www.corbis.com/

Library of Congress collection searches
http://www.loc.gov/harvest/query-lc.html

America from the Great Depression to World War II: Photographs
from the FSA [Farm Security Administration] /OWI [Office of War
Information], 1935-1945
(American Memory, Library of Congress)
http://memory.loc.gov/ammem/fsowhome.html

Great War Photos
http://www.ukans.edu/~kansite/ww_one/photos/greatwar.htm

The Major Museums of Europe commemorate the 80th anniversary
of the Armistice of 1918
http://www.art-ww1.com/

Works Progress Administration Art
(Chicago Public Schools Art Collection)
http://www.cpsart.org/wpa.lasso

The Newsfilm Library (University of South Carolina)
http://www.sc.edu/newsfilm/
Bare Bones Guide to HTML
http://werbach.com/barebones/

Copyright Website
http://www.benedict.com/

New Deal Network
http://newdeal.feri.org/

A Brief Citation Guide for Internet Sources in History and the
Humanities
(Melvin E. Page, H-Net: Humanities and Social Sciences Online)
http://www2.h-net.msu.edu/about/citation/.

United States Army Center of Military History
http://www.army.mil/cmh-pg/

Guild Press of Indiana
http://www.guildpress.com/

American Studies Crossroad Projects
(American Studies Association/Georgetown University)
http://www.georgetown.edu/crossroads/

Randy Bass. *Engines of Inquiry: A Practical Guide for Using
Technology to Teach American Culture*.
http://www.georgetown.edu/crossroads/guide/guide.html.

American Social History Project/Center for Media and Learning
(The Graduate Center, City University of New York)
http://www.ashp.cuny.edu/

New Media Classroom project (American Social History Project)
http://www.ashp.cuny.edu/index_new.html

New Media Classroom Resources
http://www.ashp.cuny.edu/nmcresources.shtml

WebBoard
http://www.webboard.com/

WebCT
http://www.webct.com/

Learning to Look: Visual Resources and the U.S. Past in the New Media Classroom http://www.ashp.cuny.edu/nmcprograms.shtml

The Visible Knowledge Project: Learning/Technology/Inquiry
http://crossroads.georgetown.edu/vkp/

Center for History and New Media (George Mason University)
http://chnm.gmu.edu/

History Matters (Center for History and New Media, George Mason University)
http://historymatters.gmu.edu/

History Departments Around the World
(George Mason University)
http://history.gmu.edu/scripts/departments.php

National Coalition for Independent Scholars
http://www.ncis.org/

National Adjunct Faculty Guild
http://www.adjunctadvocate.com/

American Historical Association
http://www.theaha.org/

Organization of American Historians
http://www.oah.org/

The Historical Society
http://www.bu.edu/historic/

Internet Resources for Students and Teachers in History

Historical Method:

Why Study History?
http://www2.tntech.edu/history/whystudy.html

A Student's Guide to the Study of History (Steven Kreis)
http://www.historyguide.org/guide/guide.html

A Student's Online Guide to History (Jules R.
Benjamin/Bedford/St. Martin's)
http://www.bedfordstmartins.com/history/benjamin/

Study Guides and Strategies (University of St. Thomas)
http://www.iss.stthomas.edu/studyguides/

The Historian's Sources (Learning Page, Library of Congress)
http://lcweb2.loc.gov/learn/lessons/psources/pshome.html

Internet for Historians (Humanities Computing Unit, Oxford
University)
http://www.humbul.ac.uk/vts/history/index.htm

Lesson Plans for History (Tennessee Tech History Web Site)
http://www2.tntech.edu/history/lesson.html

Electronic Text Center (University of Virginia)
http://etext.lib.virginia.edu/uvaonline.html
Project Gutenberg
http://www.gutenberg.net/

Online Books Page
http://digital.library.upenn.edu/books/

Computers and Audiovisual Resources in History
(Tennessee Tech History Web Site)
http://www2.tntech.edu/history/tech.html

Real Player (Real.com)
http://www.real.com/

Windows Media Player (Microsoft Corp.)
http://www.microsoft.com/windows/windowsmedia/

A Brief Citation Guide for Internet Sources in History and the
Humanities
(Melvin E. Page, H-Net: Humanities and Social Sciences
Online)
http://www2.h-net.msu.edu/about/citation/.

Libraries and Archives:

Internet Public Library
http://www.ipl.org/

LibDex: The Library Index
http://www.libdex.com/

LibWeb: Library Servers via WWW (Berkeley Digital Sunsite)
http://sunsite.berkeley.edu/Libweb/

Library of Congress
http://www.loc.gov/

British Library Public Catalogue
http://blpc.bl.uk/
New York Public Library
http://www.nypl.org/

Chicago Public Library
http://www.chipublib.org/cpl.html

WWW Virtual Library
http://vlib.org/

National Library Catalogues Worldwide
(University of Queensland, Australia)
http://www.library.uq.edu.au/ssah/jeast/

Gabriel: Gateway to Europe's National Libraries
http://portico.bl.uk/gabriel/en/welcome.html

LIBER: Ligue des Bibliotheques Europeenes de Recherche
[Association of European Research Libraries]
http://www.kb.dk/liber/

Online Library Catalogs in Asia
(East Asian Library, University of Pittsburgh)
http://www.pitt.edu/%7Eealib/libcat.htm

Universities Worldwide
(University of Innsbruck, Austria)
http://geowww.uibk.ac.at/univ/

European Archival Network
http://www.european-archival.net/

Historical Archives of the European Communities
http://wwwarc.iue.it/

NARA Archival Information Locator [NAIL] (U.S. National
Archives)
http://www.nara.gov/nara/nail.html

Historical Archives of the European Communities
http://wwwarc.iue.it/

Archives in Germany: An Introductory Guide to Institutions and
Sources
(German Historical Institute, Washington, D.C.)
http://www.ghi-dc.org/guide13/index.html

Archiespa [Archives in Spain]
http://rayuela.uc3m.es/~pirio/archiespa/

ArcheoBiblioBase: Archives in Russia
http://www.iisg.nl/~abb/

Stalin-Era Research & Archives Project (University of Toronto)
http://www.utoronto.ca/serap/

Library Catalogs and Archives (Tennessee Tech History Web Site)
http://www2.tntech.edu/history/libs.html

World History Sites:

WWW-VL: History Central Catalogue
http://www.ukans.edu/history/VL/

Academic Info: World History Gateway
http://www.academicinfo.net/hist.html

Directory of Historical Resources (History Database, Los Angeles, CA)
http://history.la.ca.us/history/hddirect.htm

Horus' Web Links to History Resources (University of California, Riverside)
http://www.ucr.edu/h-gig/horuslinks.html

Internet History Sourcebooks Project (Paul Halsall, Fordham University)
http://www.fordham.edu/halsall/

Voice of the Shuttle History Page
http://vos.ucsb.edu/shuttle/history.html

World History Association
http://www.woodrow.org/teachers/world-history/

Fernand Braudel Center (Binghamton University, SUNY)
http://fbc.binghamton.edu/

World History Center (Northeastern University)
http://www.whc.neu.edu/

World History
http://www2.tntech.edu/history/world.html

World History Archives
http://www.hartford-hwp.com/archives/

H-World (H-Net Discussion Group)
http://www2.h-net.msu.edu/~world/

Internet Global History Sourcebook (Paul Halsall, Fordham University)
http://www.fordham.edu/halsall/global/globalsbook.html

Internet Women's History Sourcebook (Paul Halsall, Fordham University)
http://www.fordham.edu/halsall/women/womensbook.html

Women in World History Curriculum (Lyn Reese)
http://www.womeninworldhistory.com/

Internet Modern History Sourcebook (Paul Halsall, Fordham University)
http://www.fordham.edu/halsall/mod/modsbook.html

History Resource Center: Modern World (The Gale Group)
http://www.galegroup.com/modernworld/

History of Western Civilization Sites:

General:

Institute of Historical Research (University of London)
http://ihr.sas.ac.uk/

WWW VL EUI European History Project
http://vlib.iue.it/history/europe.html

Index of Historical Journals (Universitat de Valencia)
http://www.uv.es/~apons/revistes.htm

History Online: The Heart of British and World History Online
http://historyonline.chadwyck.co.uk/

History of European Women
http://www.historyeuropeanwomen.com/

Ancient History:

Internet Ancient History Sourcebook (Paul Halsall, Fordham University)
http://www.fordham.edu/halsall/ancient/asbook.html

Academic Info: Ancient History
http://www.academicinfo.net/histanc.html

Academic Info: Classical Studies
http://www.academicinfo.net/classics.html

Ancient Historians in the USA
(1998 Association of Ancient Historians directory edited by Konrad H. Kinzl)
http://www.trentu.ca/ahc/aahdir.html

Argos: Limited Area Search of the Ancient and Medieval Internet
(University of Evansville)
http://argos.evansville.edu/

Centre for the Study of Ancient Documents (Oxford University)
http://www.csad.ox.ac.uk/index.html

ABZU: Guide to Resources for the Study of the Ancient Near East
Available on the Internet (Oriental Institute, University of Chicago)
http://www-oi.uchicago.edu/OI/DEPT/RA/ABZU/ABZU.HTML

Exploring Ancient World Cultures (University of Evansville)
http://eawc.evansville.edu/index.htm

Egyptology Resources (University of Cambridge, U.K.)
http://www.newton.cam.ac.uk/egypt/

The Ancient Greek World
(University of Pennsylvania Museum of Archaeology and Anthropology)
http://www.museum.upenn.edu/Greek_World/Index.html

Diotima: Materials for the Study of Women and Gender in the Ancient World
(Ross Scaife and Suzanne Bonefas)
http://www.stoa.org/diotima/

Perseus Digital Library
(Gregory Crane, Tufts University)
http://www.perseus.tufts.edu/

Byzantium: Byzantine Studies on the Internet
(Paul Halsall, Fordham University)
http://www.fordham.edu/halsall/byzantium/

Bibliography on Women in Byzantium
(Thalia Gouma-Peterson, Wooster College)
http://www.wooster.edu/ART/wb.html

Medieval History:

WWW Virtual Library History Index: Medieval Europe
http://www.msu.edu/~georgem1/history/medieval.htm

Internet Medieval Sourcebook (Paul Halsall, Fordham University)
http://www.fordham.edu/halsall/sbook.html

The Labyrinth: Resources for Medieval Studies (Georgetown University)
http://www.georgetown.edu/labyrinth/labyrinth-home.html

NetSERF: The Internet Connection for Medieval Resources
(Catholic University of America)
http://www.netserf.org/

ORB: The Online Reference Book for Medieval Studies
(Rhodes College)
http://orb.rhodes.edu/

Medieval Feminist Index (Haverford College)
http://www.haverford.edu/library/reference/mschaus/mfi/mfi.html

LIBRO: Library of Iberian Resources Online
(American Academy of Research Historians of Medieval Spain and
University of Central Arkansas)
http://libro.uca.edu/

Early Modern History:

Medieval and Renaissance Europe—Primary Historical Documents
(EuroDocs, Brigham Young University)
http://library.byu.edu/~rdh/eurodocs/medren.html

MRTS: Medieval Texts and Studies (University of Arizona)
http://www.asu.edu/clas/acmrs/mrts/home.html

ITER: Gateway to the Middle Age and Renaissance
(University of Toronto)
http://iter.utoronto.ca/

Academic Info: Renaissance History
http://www.academicinfo.net/histren.html

The Italian Renaissance (primary documents from Hanover College)
http://history.hanover.edu/early/italren.htm

Society for Renaissance Studies
http://www.sas.ac.uk/srs/

Renaissance Society of America
http://www.r-s-a.org/

Electronic Resources for Research
(Centre for Reformation and Renaissance Studies, University of Toronto)
http://www.library.utoronto.ca/crrs/Databases/WWW/Bookmarks.html

Reformation Europe (Internet Modern History Sourcebook)
http://www.fordham.edu/halsall/mod/modsbook02.html

The Protestant Reformation and The Catholic Reformation
(primary source documents from Hanover College)
http://history.hanover.edu/early/prot.html
http://history.hanover.edu/early/cath.htm

International Seminar on the History of the Atlantic World
(Bernard Bailyn, Harvard University)
http://www.fas.harvard.edu/~atlantic/index.html

Eighteenth-Century Resources—History
(Jack Lynch, Rutgers University, Newark)
http://andromeda.rutgers.edu/~jlynch/18th/history.html

Romantic Chronology [1642-1851]
(Alan Liu and Laura Mandell, University of California, Santa
Barbara)
http://www.english.ucsb.edu:591/rchrono/

Romantic Circles (University of Maryland)
http://www.rc.umd.edu/

Modern History:

Internet Modern History Sourcebook (Paul Halsall, Fordham
University)
http://www.fordham.edu/halsall/mod/modsbook.html

Modern World History (BBC Education)
http://www.bbc.co.uk/education/modern/

Liberty, Equality, Fraternity: Exploring the French Revolution
(Center for History and New Media, George Mason University)
http://chnm.gmu.edu/revolution/

Napoleon (Napoleon Foundation)
http://www.napoleon.org/

Napoleon Bonaparte Internet Guide
http://www.napoleonbonaparte.nl/

The Napoleonic Guide
http://www.napoleonguide.com/

From Marx to Mao
http://www.marx2mao.org/

Learning and Teaching About the History of Europe in the 20th Century
http://culture.coe.fr/hist20/

Alexander Palace: Everyday Life in a Romanov Palace
http://www.alexanderpalace.org/palace/

Russian and East European History
(Tennessee Tech History Web Site)
http://www2.tntech.edu/history/russee.html

World War I: An Internet History of the Great War
http://www.worldwar1.com/

WWI: The World War I Document Archive (Brigham Young University)
http://www.lib.byu.edu/~rdh/wwi/

Photos of the Great War: World War One Image Archive
http://www.ukans.edu/~kansite/ww_one/photos/greatwar.htm

The Great War and the Shaping of the 20th Century (PBS)
http://www.pbs.org/greatwar/

Age of Anxiety: The Inter-War Years (Internet Modern History Sourcebook)
http://www.fordham.edu/halsall/mod/modsbook40.html

Italian Life Under Fascism (University of Wisconsin, Madison)
http://www.library.wisc.edu/libraries/dpf/Fascism/Home.html

Links of Interest to Historians of Germany (H-German, H-Net network)
http://www2.h-net.msu.edu/~german/research/links.html

The Weimar Republic and National Socialism
(Internet Modern History Sourcebook)
http://www.fordham.edu/halsall/mod/modsbook43.html

Report of Court Proceedings: The Case of the Trotskyite-
Zinovievite
Terrorist Center [Moscow Trials of August 19-24,1936]
http://art-bin.com/art/omoscowtoc.html

The Commissar Vanishes: The Falsification of Photographs in
Stalin's Russia
(Newseum)
http://www.newseum.org/berlinwall/commissar_vanishes/

Southwark Spanish Civil War Collection (University of
California, San Diego)
http://orpheus.ucsd.edu/speccoll/collects/southw.html

World War II Links on the Internet (University of California,
San Diego)
http://history.acusd.edu/gen/ww2_links.html

World War II Resources on the Internet (Miami University)
http://www.lib.muohio.edu/inet/subj/history/wwii/

United States Holocaust Memorial Museum
http://www.ushmm.org/

Fortunoff Video Archive for Holocaust Testimonies (Yale
University)
http://www.library.yale.edu/testimonies/homepage.html

Survivors of the Shoah (Visual History Foundation)
http://www.vhf.org/

About the United Nations
http://www.un.org/aboutun/history.htm

Contemporary History:

Harvard Project on Cold War Studies
http://www.fas.harvard.edu/~hpcws/

Cold War (CNN Perspectives Series)
http://www.cnn.com/SPECIALS/cold.war/

Cold War International History Project
(Woodrow Wilson International Center for Scholars)
http://cwihp.si.edu/

WWW Virtual Library: International Affairs Resources
http://www.etown.edu/vl/

International Studies and International Sites
(Tennessee Tech History Web Site)
http://www2.tntech.edu/history/intl.html

Country Studies (Library of Congress)
http://lcweb2.loc.gov/frd/cs/cshome.html

Center for World Indigenous Studies
http://www.cwis.org/

World Factbook (U.S. Central Intelligence Agency)
http://www.cia.gov/cia/publications/factbook/

Institute of Contemporary British History (University of London)
http://ihr.sas.ac.uk/icbh/

RedIRIS: Spanish National Research Network
http://www.rediris.es/

Contemporary Portugese Politics and History Research Centre
http://www.cphrc.org.uk/

International History Sites by Geographical Area:

Asian History:

Asian Studies WWW Virtual Library (Australian National
University)
http://coombs.anu.edu.au/WWWVL-AsianStudies.html

Southeast Asian Archive (University of California, Riverside)
http://www.lib.uci.edu/rrsc/sasian.html

The Asia Society
http://www.asiasociety.org/

Asian Division, Area Studies (Library of Congress)
http://lcweb.loc.gov/rr/asian/

East Asian Library (University of Pittsburgh)
http://www.pltt.edu/~ealib/index.html

H-Asia: Asian History and Studies (H-Net)
http://www2.h-net.msu.edu/~asia/

Fifty Years of [Indian] Freedom (Rediff On The Net)
http://www.rediff.com/freedom/freedom.htm

Internet Indian History Sourcebook (Paul Halsall, Fordham University)
http://www.fordham.edu/halsall/india/indiasbook.html

Afghan History (Afghanistan Online)
http://www.afghan-web.com/history/

Documenting a Democracy: Australia's Story
http://www.foundingdocs.gov.au/home.htm

Academic Info: Australian History Page
http://www.academicinfo.net/histaus.html

H-ANZAU Mailing List (H-Net)
http://www.h-net.msu.edu/~anzau/

Electronic Journal of Australian and New Zealand History
http://www.jcu.edu.au/aff/history/

Academic Info: Chinese Studies: Chinese History
http://www.academicinfo.net/chinahist.html

Chinese Cultural Studies: Bibliographical Guide
(Paul Halsall, Brooklyn College, SUNY)
http://acc6.its.brooklyn.cuny.edu/~phalsall/chinbib.html

Chinese History Research Site (University of California, San Diego)
http://orpheus.ucsd.edu/chinesehistory/

John Fairbank Memorial Chinese History Virtual Library
http://www.cnd.org/fairbank/

History: Chinese Culture (About.com)
http://chineseculture.about.com/cs/history/index.html

History of China (Leon Poon)
http://www-chaos.umd.edu/history/toc.html

Chinese Biographical Database
(Marilyn A. Levine, Lewis-Clark State College)
http:// exodus.lcsc.edu/cbiouser

The Chairman Smiles: Posters from the former Soviet Union, Cuba and China (International Institute of Social History)
http://www.iisg.nl/exhibitions/chairman/

Virtual Museum of the "Cultural Revolution" (China News Digest)
http://www.cnd.org/CR/english/

The Gate of Heavenly Peace [Tiananmen Square, June 1989] (Frontline/PBS)
http://www.pbs.org/wgbh/pages/frontline/gate/

Tiananmen Square, 1989: The Declassified History
(National Security Archives, George Washington University)
http://www.gwu.edu/~nsarchiv/NSAEBB/NSAEBB16/

China Statistical Network
http://www.stats.gov.cn/english/index.html

Hong Kong '97: Lives in Transition (PBS)
http://www.pbs.org/pov/hongkong/

J Guide: Stanford Guide to Japan Information Resources
http://fuji.stanford.edu/jguide/

Japanese Studies Resources (East Asian Collection, Duke University Libraries)
http://www.lib.duke.edu/ias/eac/japanesestudies.html

H-JAPAN Mailing List (H-Net)
http://www2.h-net.msu.edu/~japan/

The Tokugawa Art Museum [Tokugawa period, ca. 1603-1868]
http://www.cjn.or.jp/tokugawa/index-j.html

Online Documentary: The Nanking Atrocities
(Masato Kajimoto, University of Missouri)
http://web.missouri.edu/~jschool/nanking

Germ War and Experiments on Humans (University of Minnesota)
http://www-users.cs.umn.edu/~dyue/wiihist/germwar/

Okinawa: The American Years, 1946-1972
(Nicholas E. Sarantakes, Texas A & M University)
http://www.tamu-commerce.edu/coas/history/sarantakes/Okinawa.html

NTT Japan Window
http://www.jwindow.net/

Institute of Social Science (University of Tokyo)
http://www.iss.u-tokyo.ac.jp/

Japan Policy Research Institute
http://www.jpri.org/

The Korea Institute (Harvard University)
http://www.fas.harvard.edu/~korea/index_home.html

Korean History (Korean Studies at Univ. of California, Berkeley)
http://ist-socrates.berkeley.edu/~korea/history.html

The History of Korea (Radio Korea International, Korean Broadcasting
System and National Institute for International Education Development,
Ministry of Education of Korea)
http://rki.kbs.co.kr/English/history/hok_1.html

Harvard Korean Studies Bibliography
http://www.fas.harvard.edu/~korbib/

Korean Heritage Project (University of Southern California)
http://www.usc.edu/isd/locations/ssh/korean/

Korean History Project
http://www.koreanhistoryproject.org/

Kasaysayan: Philippine History 101 (Tribung Pinoy)
http://www.tribo.org/history.html

Indonesia: Society and Culture, World Wide Web Virtual Library
(Australian National University)
http://coombs.anu.edu.au/WWWVLPages/IndonPages/WWW
VL-Indonesia.html

World Wide Web Virtual Library: Papua New Guinea
(Australian National University)
http://coombs.anu.edu.au/SpecialProj/PNG/Index.htm

South Asia Resource Access on the Internet [SARAI]
(Columbia University)
http://www.columbia.edu/cu/libraries/indiv/area/sarai/

World Wide Web Virtual Library: Socialist Republic of Vietnam
(Australian National University)
http://coombs.anu.edu.au/WWWVLPages/VietPages/WWWVL
-Vietnam.html

Vietnam War Bibliography (Edwin E. Moise, Clemson
University)
http://hubcap.clemson.edu/~eemoise/bibliography.html

The Wars for Vietnam: 1945 to 1975 (Vassar College)
http://students.vaxchssar.edu/~vietnam/

Cambodian Genocide Program (Yale University)
http://www.yale.edu/cgp/

African History:

African Studies Association
http://www.africanstudies.org/

H-Africa (H-Net)
http://www2.h-net.msu.edu/~africa/

H-SAfrica (H-Net)
http://www2.h-net.msu.edu/~safrica/

H-AfrTeach (H-Net)
http://www2.h-net.msu.edu/~afrteach/

H-AfResearch: Research in African Primary Sources (H-Net)
http://www2.h-net.msu.edu/~afrsrch/

Journal of African History
http://uk.cambridge.org/journals/afh/

Internet African History Sourcebook (Paul Halsall, Fordham University)
http://www.fordham.edu/halsall/africa/africasbook.html

South African university history departments (Yenza!)
http://www.nrf.ac.za/yenza/links/history.htm

African Academic Resources (Pier Larson, Johns Hopkins University)
http://jhunix.hcf.jhu.edu/~plarson/main/links/aac.html

South African Data Archives
(Human Sciences Research Council, Pretoria, South Africa)
http://www.hsrc.ac.za/sada.html

Africa South of the Sahara: Selected Internet Resources
(Karen Fung, Stanford University)
http://www-sul.stanford.edu/depts/ssrg/africa/guide.html
The History of Ghana
http://www.uta.fi/~csfraw/ghana/general/gh_hist.html

Africa Action
http://www.africapolicy.org/index.shtml

Association of Concerned Africa Scholars
http://www.prairienet.org/acas/

Canadian History:

Canadian Historical Association
http://www.cha-shc.ca/

Association for Canadian Studies
http://www.acs-aec.ca/

Canadian Journal of History
http://www.usask.ca/history/cjh/

H-Canada: Canadian History and Studies (H-Net)
http://www2.h-net.msu.edu/~canada/

WWW-VL History: Canadian History
http://www.ukans.edu/history/VL/CANADA/canada.html

Canadian History on the Web (Dr. Susan Neylan)
http://members.home.net/dneylan/index.html

Canadian History and Studies
(Tennessee Tech History Web Site)
http://www2.tntech.edu/history/canada.html

The Canadian Encyclopedia
http://www.thecanadianencyclopedia.com/

Canadian Archival Resources on the Internet
(University of Saskatchewan)
http://www.usask.ca/archives/menu.html
Latin American History:

Latin American Studies Association
http://lasa.international.pitt.edu/

Latin American Network Information Center (University of Texas)
http://info.lanic.utexas.edu/

Handbook of Latin American Studies (HLAS) Online (U.S. Library of Congress)
http://lcweb2.loc.gov/hlas/

Political Database of the Americas (Georgetown University/OAS)
http://www.georgetown.edu/pdba/

Latin American Government Documents Project (Cornell University)
http://lib1.library.cornell.edu/colldev/ladocshome.html

Resources for Teaching about the Americas (RETAnet)
http://ladb.unm.edu/retanet/

Institute of History (Catholic University, Santiago, Chile)
http://www.hist.puc.cl/historia/

PROFMEX: Worldwide Network for Research on Mexico
http://www.isop.ucla.edu/profmex/

Mystery of the Maya (Canadian Museum of Civilization)
http://www.civilization.ca/membrs/civiliz/maya/mminteng.html

Abya Yala Net (South and Meso American Indian Rights Center)
http://abyayala.nativeweb.org/

Centro de Pesquisa e Documentação de História Contemporânea do Brasil
http://www.cpdoc.fgv.br/comum/htm/

Middle East History:

Middle East Studies Internet Resources (Columbia University Libraries)
http://www.columbia.edu/cu/lweb/indiv/mideast/cuvlm/index.html

Middle East Studies Association
http://w3fp.arizona.edu/mesassoc/index.html

Encyclopedia of the Orient (CIAS/Centre d'Information Arabe Scandinave)
http://lexicorient.com/e.o/index.htm

Persian History (Persia.Net)
http://www.persianweb.com/history.html

Oxford Centre for Islamic Studies (Oxford University, U.K.)
http://www.oxcis.ac.uk/

Turkish Studies Association
http://bsuvc.bsu.edu/~tsa/

Armenian Research Center (University of Michigan, Dearborn)
http://www.umd.umich.edu/dept/armenian/

Internet Islamic History Sourcebook (Paul Halsall, Fordham University)
http://www.fordham.edu/halsall/islam/islamsbook.html

Palestine in the 1930s: A Photo Essay
http://www.snunit.k12.il/museum/pal/Palestine.html

Internet Jewish History Sourcebook (Paul Halsall, Fordham University)
http://www.fordham.edu/halsall/jewish/jewishsbook.html

YIVO Institute for Jewish Research (New York, NY)
http://www.yivoinstitute.org/

Yad Vashem: The Holocaust Martyrs' and Heroes'
Remembrance Authority
http://www.yadvashem.org.il/

Jewish Internet Portal (HaReshima)
http://www.hareshima.com/culture/History.asp

Israel at 50 (New York Times)
http://www.nytimes.com/library/world/israel-index.html

Question of Palestine: History (United Nations)
http://www.un.org/Depts/dpa/ngo/history.html

Palestinian Academic Society for the Study of International
Affairs
http://www.passia.org/

Guide to Palestinian Web sites (Birzeit University)
http://www.birzeit.edu/links/

United States History:

General:

WWW-VL History: United States
http://www.ukans.edu/history/VL/USA/index.html

Academic Info: United States History Resources
http://www.academicinfo.net/histus.html

National Museum of American History (Smithsonian Institution)
http://americanhistory.si.edu/

America's Story from America's Library (Library of Congress)
http://www.americaslibrary.gov/

Pluralism and Unity (H-Net and Michigan State University)
http://www.expo98.msu.edu/

American Memory: Historical Collections for the National Digital Library (Library of Congress)
http://memory.loc.gov/

Words and Deeds in American History (Library of Congress)
http://memory.loc.gov/ammem/mcchtml/corhome.html

Core Documents of U.S. Democracy (U.S. Superintendent of Documents)
http://www.access.gpo.gov/su_docs/locators/coredocs/index.html

POTUS: Presidents of the United States (Internet Public Library)
http://www.ipl.org/ref/POTUS/

The Presidents (The American Experience, PBS)
http://www.pbs.org/wgbh/amex/presidents/indexjs.html

Presidents (Inaugural, State of the Union and Farewell addresses)
http://odur.let.rug.nl/~usa/P/

President (links to presidential libraries)
http://www.ibiblio.org/lia/president/

U.S. Senate Historical Office
http://www.senate.gov/learning/learn_history_about.html

Historical Highlights (Office of the Clerk, U.S. House of Representatives)
http://clerkweb.house.gov/histrecs/history.htm

Congressional Archives (Carl Albert Congressional Research and Studies Center, University of Oklahoma)
http://www.ou.edu/special/albertctr/archives/

Douglass: Archives of American Public Address (Northwestern University)
http://douglass.speech.nwu.edu/

U.S. Supreme Court Opinions (FindLaw for Legal Professionals)
http://www.findlaw.com/10fedgov/judicial/supreme_court/opinions.html

Famous Trials (Doug Linder, University of Missouri, Kansas City Law School)
http://www.law.umkc.edu/faculty/projects/ftrials/ftrials.htm

Hypertexts (University of Virginia)
http://xroads.virginia.edu/~HYPER/hypertex.html

Avalon Project: Documents in Law, History and Diplomacy (Yale Law School)
http://www.yale.edu/lawweb/avalon/avalon.htm

Making of America (University of Michigan)
http://moa.umdl.umich.edu/)

Chronology of U.S. Historical Documents (University of Oklahoma College of Law)
http://www.law.ou.edu/hist/

History Resource Center: U.S. (The Gale Group)
http://www.galegroup.com/HistoryRC/index.htm

Bibliographies in Women's History and Studies (University of Maryland)
http://www.inform.umd.edu/EdRes/Topic/WomensStudies/Bibliographies/

U.S. Diplomatic History
http://www2.tntech.edu/diplo.html

African American History and Studies
http://www2.tntech.edu/history/black.html

Economic History
http://www2.tntech.edu/history/economic.html

Environmental History
http://www2.tntech.edu/history/envir.html

Gender History and Studies
http://www2.tntech.edu/gender.html

Labor History
http://www2.tntech.edu/labor.html

Military History
http://www2.tntech.edu/military.html

Native American History and Studies
http://www2.tntech.edu/history/nativam.html

History of Science and Technology
http://www2.tntech.edu/history/scitech.html

Southern History
http://www2.tntech.edu/history/south.html

State and Local History
http://www2.tntech.edu/history/state.html

Doing Oral History
http://www2.tntech.edu/history/oral.html

ECHO: Exploring and Collecting History Online, Science and
Technology
(Center for History and New Media, George Mason University)
http://chnm.gmu.edu/echo/

American Studies Sites:

American Studies Association
http://www.georgetown.edu/crossroads/asainfo.html

Popular Culture Association/ American Culture Association
http://www2.h-net.msu.edu/~pcaaca/

British Association for American Studies
http://www.baas.ac.uk/

American Studies Center, Salzburg Seminar, Austria
http://www.salzburgseminar.org/intro.cfm?status=programs

U.S. History to 1800:

Ancient Mesoamerican Civilizations
(Kevin L. Callahan, University of Minnesota)
http://www.angelfire.com/ca/humanorigins/index.html

Columbus and the Age of Discovery (Millersville University)
http://muweb.millersv.edu/~columbus/

Omohundro Institute for Early American History and Culture
http://www.wm.edu/oieahc/

H-OIEAHC Links
(Omhoundro Institute for Early American History and Culture)
http://www2.h-net.msu.edu/~ieahcweb/links/

Virtual Jamestown (Virginia Center for Digital History,
University of Virginia)
http://jefferson.village.virginia.edu/vcdh/jamestown/

Museum of African Slavery (Pier M. Larson, Johns Hopkins
University)
http://jhunix.hcf.jhu.edu/~plarson/smuseum/welcome.htm

Africans in American (PBS)
http://www.pbs.org/wgbh/aia/home.html

Benjamin Franklin: A Documentary History
(J.A. Leo Lemay, University of Delaware)
http://www.english.udel.edu/lemay/franklin/

A Midwife's Tale: Eighteenth Century America Through a
Woman's Eyes (The American Experience, PBS)
http://www.pbs.org/wgbh/amex/midwife/

Liberty! The American Revolution (PBS)
http://www.pbs.org/ktca/liberty/

The American Revolution: National Discussion of Our
Revolutionary Origins (H-Net: Humanities and Social Sciences
Online)
http://revolution.h-net.msu.edu/

Constitution Day [September 17, 1787] (National Archives)
http://www.nara.gov/education/teaching/constitution/home.html

National Constitution Center (Philadelphia, PA)
http://www.constitutioncenter.org/

The Illustrating Traveler: Adventure and Illustration in North
America and the Caribbean, 1760-1895 (Yale University)
http://www.library.yale.edu/beinecke/illus.htm

United States Historical Census Data Browser [1790-1960]
(University of Virginia)
http://fisher.lib.virginia.edu/census/

!9th Century U.S. History:

A History of American Agriculture (U.S. Department of
Agriculture)
http://www.usda.gov/history2/

Core Historical Literature of Agriculture (Cornell University)
http://chla.library.cornell.edu/

Whole Cloth: Discovering Science and Technology Through
American History (Smithsonian Institution)
http://www.si.edu/lemelson/centerpieces/whole_cloth/

"Tales of the Early Republic" (Hal Morris)
http://216.202.17.223/index.html

Antebellum American History, 1812-1864
(University of Colorado)
http://web.uccs.edu/~history/index/antebellum.html

Brief History of the Trail of Tears (Cherokee Messenger)
http://www.neosoft.com/powersource/cherokee/history.html

Women and Social Movements in the United States, 1820-1940 (Binghamton University, SUNY)
http://womhist.binghamton.edu/

Interpreting the Irish Famine, 1846-1850 (University of Virginia)
http://www.people.virginia.edu/~eas5e/Irish/Famine.html

Views of the Famine (Vassar College)
http://vassun.vassar.edu/~sttaylor/FAMINE/

Tangled Roots: A Project Exploring the Histories of Americans of Irish Heritage and Americans of African Heritage (Yale University)
http://www.yale.edu/glc/tangledroots/

Center for the Study of Southern Culture (University of Mississippi)
http://www.olemiss.edu/depts/south/index.html

Documenting the American South (University of North Carolina)
http://docsouth.unc.edu/

Southern Historical Collection (University of North Carolina)
http://www.lib.unc.edu/mss/shcgl.html

Gilder Lehrman Institute of American History [history of slavery]
http://vi.uh.edu/pages/mintz/GILDER.htm

Born in Slavery: Slave Narratives from the Federal Writers' Project, 1936-1938 (Library of Congress)
http://memory.loc.gov/ammem/snhtml/

American Slave Narratives: An Online Anthology (University of Virginia)
http://xroads.virginia.edu/~hyper/wpa/wpahome.html

American Slavery: A Composite Autobiography (Greenwood Publishing Group)
http://www.slavenarratives.com/

African-American Religion: A Documentary History Project (Amherst College)
http://www.amherst.edu/~aardoc/menu.html

African-American Women Writers of the 19th Century (Digital Schomburg)
http://digital.nypl.org/schomburg/writers_aa19/

Amistad Research Center (Tulane University)
http://www.tulane.edu/~amistad/

The African-American Mosaic: A Library of Congress Resource Guide for the Study of Black History and Culture
http://lcweb.loc.gov/exhibits/african/intro.html

Taking the Train to Freedom: Underground Railroad, Special Resource Study (National Park Service)
http://www.nps.gov/undergroundrr/contents.htm

Influence of Prominent Abolitionists
(African-American Mosaic, Library of Congress)
http://memory.loc.gov/ammem/vfwhtml/vfwhome.html

The Mexican-American War Memorial Homepage
(Universidad Nacional Autónoma de México)
http://sunsite.dcaa.unam.mx/revistas/1847/

"Votes for Women" Suffrage Pictures, 1850-1920 (Library of Congress)
http://memory.loc.gov/ammem/vfwhtml/vfwhome.html

E Pluribus Unum: An Online Archive of 1850s America (Assumption College)
http://www.assumption.edu/ahc/default1850.html

The Dred Scott Case (Washington University Libraries)
http://www.library.wustl.edu/vlib/dredscott/

Nineteenth Century Documents Project (Lloyd Benson,
Furman University)
http://www.furman.edu/~benson/docs/

Civil War Resources on the Internet: Abolitionism to
Reconstruction, 1830s-1890s (Rutgers University)
http://www.libraries.rutgers.edu/rul/rr_gateway/research_guide
s/history/civwar.sthml

United States Civil War Center (Louisiana State University)
http://www.cwc.lsu.edu/

The American Civil War Homepage
(George H. Hoemann, University of Tennessee)
http://sunsite.utk.edu/civil-war/warweb.html

The Civil War: The American Battlefield Protection Program
(ParkNet, National Park Service)
http://www2.cr.nps.gov/abpp/civil.htm#parks

Civil War Maps (Library of Congress)
http://lcweb2.loc.gov/ammem/gmdhtml/cwmhtml/

Civil War Soldiers & Sailors System (National Park Service)
http://www.civilwar.nps.gov/cwss/

The Fight for Equal Rights: Black Soldiers in the Civil War
(National Archives)
http://www.nara.gov/education/teaching/usct/home.html

Civil War Women: Online Archival Collections (Duke
University)
http://scriptorium.lib.duke.edu/collections/civil-war-women.html

Freedmen and Southern Society Project (University of
Maryland)
http://www.inform.umd.edu/EdRes/Colleges/ARHU/Depts/Hist
ory/Freedman/home.html

Toward Racial Equality: *Harper's Weekly* Reports on Black America, 1857-1874
http://blackhistory.harpweek.com/

Impeachment 1868/1999 (History Matters, Center for History and New Media)
http://historymatters.gmu.edu/impeach.html

Finding Precedent: Hayes v. Tilden
The Electoral College Controversy of 1876-1877 (HarpWeek)
http://elections.harpweek.com/controversy.htm

New Perspectives on the West (PBS)
http://www.pbs.org/weta/thewest/

Western History Association
http://www.unm.edu/~wha/

Western Historical Quarterly
http://www.usu.edu/~history/whq/

WestWeb (Catherine Lavender, College of Staten Island, CUNY)
http://www.library.csi.cuny.edu/westweb/

American Heritage Center (University of Wyoming)
http://uwadmnweb.uwyo.edu/ahc/

H-SHGAPE Internet Resources (Gilded Age and Progressive Era)
http://www2.h-net.msu.edu/~shgape/internet/

Journal of the Gilded Age and Progressive Era
http://www.jgape.org/

The American 1890s: A Chronology (Bowling Green State University)
http://www.bgsu.edu/departments/acs/1890s/america.html

Explore Your Family History at Ellis Island
(American Family Immigration History Center)
http://www.ellisisland.org/

Port of Entry: Immigration Teacher Material (National Archives)
http://lcweb2.loc.gov/learn/activity/port/teacher.html

1896: The Presidential Campaign, Cartoons & Commentary (Rebecca Edwards and Sarah DeFeo, Vassar College)
http://iberia.vassar.edu/1896/1896home.html

The Era of William McKinley (K. Austin Kerr, Ohio State University)
http://www.history.ohio-state.edu/projects/mckinley/default.htm

The World of 1898: The Spanish-American War (Library of Congress)
http://lcweb.loc.gov/rr/hispanic/1898/index.html

Centennial of the War of 1898
(Centro de Estudios Norteamericanos, Universidad de Alcalá)
http://www2.alcala.es/1898/

20th Century U.S. History:

Between a Rock and a Hard Place:
A History of American Sweatshops, 1820 to the Present
(National Museum of American History, Smithsonian Institution)
http://memory.loc.gov/ammem/amrvhtml/conshome.html

In the Shadow of the I.W.W. (Walter P. Reuther Library, Wayne State University)
http://www.reuther.wayne.edu/exhibits/iww.html

Publications by the Industrial Workers of the World (University of Arizona)
http://digital.library.arizona.edu/bisbee/main/iww.php

Theodore Roosevelt: His Life and Times on Film
(American Memory, Library of Congress)
http://memory.loc.gov/ammem/trfhtml/

Evolution of the Conservation Movement, 1850-1920 (Library of Congress)
http://memory.loc.gov/ammem/amrvhtml/conshome.html

1912: Competing Visions for America (Ohio State University)
http://1912.history.ohio-state.edu/default.htm

Temperance & Prohibition (K. Austin Kerr, Ohio State University)
http://www.history.ohio-state.edu/projects/prohibition/Contents.htm

Woman Suffrage and the 19th Amendment (National Archives)
http://www.nara.gov/education/teaching/woman/home.html

W.E.B. Du Bois Institute for Afro-American Research (Harvard University)
http://web-dubois.fas.harvard.edu/

Western Front Association, USA
http://www.wfa-usa.org/new/index.cfm

The War with Germany: A Statistical Summary (Col. Leonard P. Ayres, 1919)
http://www.ukans.edu/~kansite/ww_one/docs/statistics/statstc.htm

Sow the Seeds of Victory! Posters from the Food Administration During World War I (National Archives)
http://www.nara.gov/education/cc/foodww1.html

Red Scare, 1918-1921 (Baruch College, CUNY)
http://newman.baruch.cuny.edu/digital/redscare/default.htm
Sacco-Vanzetti Case (University of Pennsylvania)
http://www.english.upenn.edu/~afilreis/88/sacvan.html

The Volstead Act and Related Prohibition Documents (National Archives)
http://www.nara.gov/education/cc/foodww1.html

Marcus Garvey: Look for Me in the Whirlwind (American Experience, PBS)
http://www.pbs.org/wgbh/amex/garvey/

Marcus Garvey and Universal Negro Improvement Association Papers Project (UCLA)
http://www.isop.ucla.edu/mgpp/

Prosperity and Thrift: The Coolidge Era and the Consumer Economy, 1921-1929 (American Memory, Library of Congress)
http://memory.loc.gov/ammem/coolhtml/coolhome.html

The 1920s (University of Louisville)
http://www.louisville.edu/~kprayb01/1920s.html

Tennessee vs. John Scopes: The "Monkey Trial" 1925 (Famous Trials in American History, Univ. of Missouri, Kansas City Law School)
http://www.law.umkc.edu/faculty/projects/ftrials/scopes/scopes.htm

Harlem: Mecca of the New Negro (*Survey Graphic*, March 1925)
http://etext.lib.virginia.edu/harlem/

Schomburg Center for Research in Black Culture (New York Public Library)
http://www.nypl.org/research/sc/sc.html

The Great Depression (1993 film series by Blackside Films)
http://www2.blackside.com/blackside/BlacksideFilms/Depressionfilm.html

New Deal Network (Franklin and Eleanor Roosevelt Institute/Columbia Univ.)
http://newdeal.feri.org/

America from the Great Depression to World War II:
Black and White Photographs from the FSA-OWI, 1935-1945
http://memory.loc.gov/ammem/fsahtml/fahome.html

American Life Histories: Manuscripts from the Federal Writers' Project, 1936-1940 (American Memory, Library of Congress)
http://lcweb2.loc.gov/wpaintro/wpahome.html

America in the 1930's (American Studies Program, University of Virginia)
http://xroads.virginia.edu/~1930s/DISPLAY/displayframe.html

History Page (Social Security Online)
http://www.ssa.gov/history/history.html

"Been Here So Long:" Selections from the WPA Slave Narratives (New Deal Network)
http://newdeal.feri.org/asn/index.htm

Southern Oral History Program (University of North Carolina)
http://www.sohp.org/

Remembering Pearl Harbor, December 7, 1941 (National Geographic Society)
http://plasma.nationalgeographic.com/pearlharbor/

World War II Links on the Internet (University of San Diego)
http://history.acusd.edu/gen/ww2_links.html

World War II Resources on the Internet (Miami University)
http://www.lib.muohio.edu/inet/subj/history/wwii/

National D-Day Museum (New Orleans, LA)
http://www.ddaymuseum.org/home.htm

Links to Other Resources (Relocation of Japanese-Americans on home front) (National Japanese American Memorial Foundation)
http://www.njamf.org/

The High Energy Weapons Archive: A Guide to Nuclear Weapons
http://www.fas.org/nuke/hew/

Enola Gay (former exhibition)
(National Air and Space Museum, Smithsonian Institution)
http://www.nasm.edu/galleries/gal103/

The Enola Gay and the Smithsonian
([U.S.] Air Force Association)
http://www.afa.org/enolagay/home.html

Cold War (CNN Perspectives Series)
http://www.cnn.com/SPECIALS/cold.war/

Cold War International History Project
(Woodrow Wilson International Center for Scholars)
http://cwihp.si.edu/

McCarthyism (Spartacus Internet Encyclopedia)
http://www.spartacus.schoolnet.co.uk/USAred.htm

Red Files (PBS)
http://www.pbs.org/redfiles/

The Korean War (Project Whistlestop)
http://www.whistlestop.org/study_collections/korea/large/

The Fifties Web
http://www.fiftiesweb.com/fifties.htm

The Literature & Culture of the American 1950s
(Al Filreis, University of Pennsylvania)
http://dept.english.upenn.edu/~afilreis/50s/home.html

National Aeronautics and Space Administration [NASA]
History Office
http://www.hq.nasa.gov/office/pao/History/history.html

The President John F. Kennedy Assassination Records
Collection (National Archives)
http://www.nara.gov/research/jfk/

LBJ in the Oval Office (sound files from History Out Loud)
http://www.hpol.org/lbj/

Martin Luther King, Jr. Papers Project (Stanford University)
http://www.stanford.edu/group/King/

Civil Rights Documentation Project (University of Southern Mississippi)
http://www-dept.usm.edu/~mcrohb/

National Civil Rights Museum (Memphis, Tennessee)
http://www.civilrightsmuseum.org/

Free Speech Movement Digital Archive (University of California, Berkeley)
http://www.lib.berkeley.edu/BANC/FSM/

The Wars for Vietnam, 1945 to 1975 (Vassar College)
http://vassun.vassar.edu/~vietnam/

Vietnam War Bibliography (Edwin E. Moise, Clemson University)
http://hubcap.clemson.edu/~eemoise/bibliography.html

Vietnam War Internet Project
http://www.vwip.org/vwiphome.html

The Counterculture of the Sixties
http://www.geocities.com/SoHo/Studios/2914/

1969 Woodstock Festival & Concert
http://www.woodstock69.com/

The Sixties Project (University of Virginia)
http://lists.village.virginia.edu/sixties/

The Whole World Was Watching: An Oral History of 1968 (Brown University)
http://www.stg.brown.edu/projects/1968/

May 4, 1970 [shootings at Kent State University] (J. Gregory Payne, Emerson College)
http://www.emerson.edu/acadepts/cs/comm/may4.html

Documents from the Women's Liberation Movement (Duke University)
http://scriptorium.lib.duke.edu/wlm/

The Nixon Links: Now More Than Ever
http://www.geocities.com/CapitolHill/Lobby/4994/

Watergate 25 (Washington Post)
http://www.washingtonpost.com/wp-srv/national/longterm/watergate/front.htm

Society & Politics shows (PBS)
http://www.pbs.org/neighborhoods/news/

Working Familes.com: The AFL-CIO Internet Community
http://www.workingfamilies.com/

Executive Paywatch (AFL-CIO)
http://www.aflcio.org/paywatch/index.htm

The Gulf War [1991] (Frontline, PBS)
http://www.pbs.org/wgbh/pages/frontline/gulf/index.html

The Clinton Years (ABC News Nightline, Frontline, PBS)
http://abcnews.go.com/onair/nightline/clintonyears/clinton/index.html

Statistical Abstract of the United States (U.S. Census Bureau)
http://www.census.gov/statab/www/

FirstGov: Your First Click to the U.S. Government
http://www.firstgov.gov/

Almanac of American Politics (National Journal)
http://nationaljournal.com/about/almanac/

Civic Education Network (American Political Science Association)
http://www.apsanet.org/CENnet/

U.S. Election Campaign Information
http://www2.tntech.edu/history/elec.html

American Public Opinion & U.S. Foreign Policy 1999
(Chicago Council on Foreign Relations)
http://www.ccfr.org/publications/opinion/opinion.html

Pew Research Center for the People & the Press
http://www.people-press.org/

The Gallup Organization [public opinion polls]
http://www.gallup.com/

NORC [National Opinion Research Center] (University of
Chicago)
http://www.norc.uchicago.edu/

PollingReport.com
http://www.pollingreport.com/

Roper Center for Public Opinion Research (University of
Connecticut)
http://www.ropercenter.uconn.edu/

The Internet & American Life (Pew Research Center)
http://www.pewinternet.org/

CD-ROM History Projects Mentioned in This Work:

American Social History Project. Roy Rosenzweig, Roy, Steve
Brier, and Josh Brown. *Who Built America? CD-ROM: From the
Centennial Celebration of 1876 to the Great War of 1914*. New
York: Learning Technologies Interactive/Voyager CD-ROMs,
1993, 1998. Ordering information available online at
http://voyager.learntech.com/cdrom/catalogpage.cgi?wba.

American Social History Project. Roy Rosenzweig, Roy, Steve
Brier, and Josh Brown. *Who Built America? CD-ROM: From the
Centennial Celebration of 1876 to the Great War of 1914 to the
Dawn of the Atomic Age in 1946*. New York: Learning
Technologies Interactive/Voyager CD-ROMs, 2000. Ordering
information available online at http://voyager.learntech.com/
cdrom/catalogpage.cgi?wba.

Ayers, Edward L. and Anne S. Rubin. *The Eve of War. Valley of the Shadow: Two Communities in the American Civil War*. New York: W.W. Norton, 2000. Includes **CD-ROM** and book.

Brown, Thomas J. "The House Divided and Digitized." *Reviews in American History* 29 (June 2001): 205-214. Review of Edward L. Ayers and Anne S. Rubin, *The Valley of the Shadow: Two Communities in the American Civil War, Part 1: The Eve of War,* **CD-ROM** and accompanying 103 page booklet.

The Civil War CD-ROM. The War of the Rebellion: A Compilation of the Official Records of the Union and Confederate Armies. Carmel, IN: Guild Press of Indiana, 1996.

The Civil War on the Web: A Guide to the Very Best Sites, eds. William G. Thomas and Alice E. Carter. Foreword by Gary W. Gallagher. Wilmington, DE: Scholarly Resources, 2001. Includes book and **CD-ROM** by Thomas and Carter who worked with the "Valley of the Shadow" Project and the online site of the *New York Times*.

Friedheim, William. *"Who Built America?* In the Classroom." Paper delivered at the American Historical Association convention, New York, NY, January 3, 1997, available online at http://www.ashp.cuny.edu/friedheim.html, July 2001.

Kornblith, Gary J. "Venturing into the Civil War, Virtually: A Review," *Journal of American History* 88 (June 2001): 145-151. A review of "The Valley of the Shadow: Two Communities in the American Civil War" Web site at the University of Virginia led by Edward L. Ayers (http://jefferson.village.virginia.edu/vshadow2) by an experienced **multimedia** historian at Oberlin College.

Oshinsky, David M. "Web Sites with Civil War Lore Are as Popular as the Battlefields." *New York Times*, November 2, 2000. Review of *The Civil War on the Web*, eds. William G. Thomas and Alice E. Carter.

Reagan, Patrick D. **American Journey: World War I and the Jazz Age**. Farmington Hills, MI: Gale Group/Primary Source Microform, 2000. A **CD-ROM** volume in the American Journey: History in Your Hands Series. Available online at "American

Journey Online: History in Your Hands,"
http://www.americanjourney.psmedia.com/, July 2001.

Rosenzweig, Roy. "'So, What's Next for Clio?' CD-ROM and Historians." *Journal of American History* 81 (March 1995): 1621-1640. Review essay on sixteen early **CD-ROMs** with historical subject matter. Available online at the Center for History and New Media, http://chnm.gmu.edu/chnm/clio.html, July 2001.

_____, Steve Brier, and Josh Brown. *Who Built America? From the Centennial Celebration of 1876 to the Great War of* 1914. New York: Learning Technologies Interactive/Voyager CD-ROMs, 1993, 1998. Ordering information online at http://voyager.learntech.com/cdrom/catalogpage.cgi?wba.

U.S. Army. Center of Military History. *The United States Army in World War I*. Washington, D.C.: U.S. Army Center of Military History, 1998. 3 **CD-ROM** disks. Originally published in printed form 1988-1992.

Further Readings on History and the Internet

Alexander, Janet E. and Marsha Ann Tate. *Web Wisdom: How to Evaluate and Create Information Quality on the Web*. Mahwah, NJ: Lawrence Erlbaum Associates, Inc., 1999.

American Social History Project. *Who Built America? Working People and the Nation's Economy, Politics, Culture, and Society*. *Volume One: From Conquest and Colonization to 1877*. *Volume Two: 1877 to the Present*. New York: Pantheon, 1989, 1992 and revised edition, New York: Worth Publishers, 2000.

American Social History Project Center for Media and Learning. *New Media Classroom Teacher's Handbook*. Prototype Edition. New York: American Social History Project Center for Media and Learning, 2000. A manual for history teachers developed for use in the New Media Classroom project by members of the American Social History project.

Auer, Nicole J. "Bibliography on Evaluating Internet Resources." http://www.lib.vt.edu/research/libinst/evalbiblio.html, accessed July 21, 2001.

Bass, Randy. *Engines of Inquiry: A Practical Guide for Using Technology to Teach American Culture*. A Collaborative Publication of the American Studies Crossroads Project sponsored by the American Studies Project by the Crossroads Project Director online at http://www.georgetown.edu/crossroads/guide/guide.html.

Benjamin, Jules R. *A Student's Guide to History*, eighth edition. New York: Bedford/St. Martin's, 2001. Student study guide for history that includes extensive material on use of the Internet along with listings of key history Web sites by subject.

Blumenstyk. "2 Former Professors Look to Technology to Bolster Scholarly Presses' History Offering." *Chronicle of Higher Education*, http://chronicle.com. July 25, 2001.

Bush, Vannevar. "As We May Think." *Atlantic Monthly* 176 (July 1945): 101-108. Online at http://www.theatlantic.com/unbound/flashbks/computer/bushf.htm.

Carlson, Scott. "JSTOR's Journal-Archiving Service Makes Fans of Librarians and Scholars: But some worry about loss of paper copies and about cost issues." *Chronicle of Higher Education*, July 27, 2001, p. A26-28.

Chandler, Alfred D. and James W. Cortada, eds. *A Nation Transformed by Information: How Information Has Shaped the United States From Colonial Times to the Present*. New York: Oxford University Press, 2000.

"Computers and Communication Networks." Special Issue of *Business History Review* 75 (Spring 2001): 1-176.

Epstein, Jason. "Reading the Digital Future." *New York Review of Books*, July 5, 2001. Available online at http://www.nybooks.com/articles/14318.

"Essays on History and New Media." Center for History and New Media, http://chnm.gmu.edu/chnm/essays.html, July 2001.

Hafner, Katie and Matthew Lyon. *Where Wizards Stay Up Late: The Origins of the Internet*. New York: Simon & Schuster, 1996.

Himmelfarb, Gertrude. "A Neo-Luddite Reflects on the Internet." *Chronicle of Higher Education*, November 1, 1996, p. A56.

History Computer Review, semi-annual, peer-reviewed journal that publishes articles on teaching with computer technology, reviews of books, software, CD-ROMs, and Web sites; and summarizes articles in recent issues of computer magazines. Available for $20 annual subscription from Department of History, Pittsburgh State University, Pittsburg, Kansas 66762 (316) 235-4317 (fax) (316) 235-4080 or **e-mail** to jschick@pittstate.edu.

Horton, Sarah. *Web Teaching Guide: A Practical Approach to Creating Course Web Sites*. New Haven: Yale University Press, 2000.

Keating, Anne B. with Joseph Hargitai. *The Wired Professor: A Guide to Incorporating the World Wide Web in College Instruction*. New York: New York University Press, 1999.

Lynch, Patrick J. and Sarah Horton. *Web Style Guide: Basic Design Principles for Creating Web Sites*. New Haven: Yale University Press, 1999.

McMichael, Andrew; Michael O'Malley, and Roy Rosenzweig,"Historians and the Web: A Guide," *Perspectives: The American Historical Association Newsletter* 34 (January 1996): 11-15. Online at http://chnm.gmu.edu/chnm/beginner.html, July 2001.

Nelson, Lynn H. "A New Jerusalem On-Line." Unpublished paper, 2001. University of Kansas historian Nelson's thought-provoking essay is online at http://www.ukans.edu/history/ftp/internet_history/beitrag-draft/english.

O'Malley, Michael and Roy Rosenzweig. "Brave New World or Blind Alley? American History on the World Wide Web," *Journal of American History* 84 (June 1997): 137-155 available online at http://chnm.gmu.edu/chnm/jah.html, July 2001.

Page, Melvin E. "A Brief Citation Guide for Internet Sources in History and the Humanities." Online at http://www2.h-net.msu.edu/about/citation/.

Perspectives on Audiovisuals in the Teaching of History: A Collection of Essays from Perspectives, the Newsletter of the American Historical Association. Intro. By Robert Brent Toplin. Washington, D.C.: American Historical Association, 1999. Available from pubsales@theaha.org or http://www.theaha.org/.

Trachtenberg, Alan. *Reading American Photographs: Images as History, Matthew Brady to Walker Evans*. New York: Hill and Wang, 1989.

Trinkle, Dennis. *Writing, Teaching, and Researching History in the Electronic Age: Historians and Computers*. Armonk, NY: M.E. Sharpe, 1998. Fifteen essays on historians' use of computers and the Internet for research and teaching from a May 1997 conference at the University of Cincinnati.

_____ and Scott A. Merriman, eds. *History.edu: Essays on Teaching with Technology*. Armonk, NY: M.E. Sharpe, 2001. Seventeen essays, most of which grew out of annual conference of the American Association for History and Computing.

_____ and Scott A. Merriman, eds. **The History Highway 2000: A Guide to Internet Resources**, second edition. Armonk. NY: M.E. Sharpe, 2000. The most comprehensive guide to history-related sources on the Internet in a revised edition.